Chapter – 4
India's First Trick Based Study Material

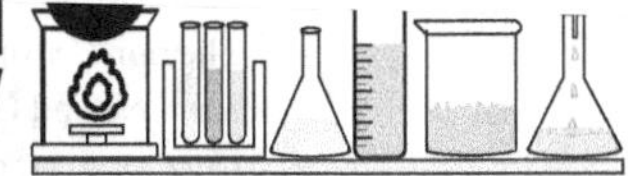

CHEMICAL BONDING

1 | ELECTRONIC THEORY OF VALENCY

The theory of valency explains chemical combination in terms of electrons. The theory was developed independently by W. Kossel and G.N. Lewis (1916) and extended by Irving Langmuir (in 1919).

The chemical behaviour of an atom is determined to a large extent by the number and arrangement of electrons in the outer orbitals of the atom. Only these electrons are involved in chemical combination and so these are called the valence electrons.

COMPLETED ELECTRON OCTET OR DUPLET

Group 0 of the periodic table contains the noble gases. With the exception of helium which has a $1s^2$ electron arrangement others have $ns^2\, np^6$ configuration in the outer orbitals.

He $\mathbf{1s^2}$
Ne $1s^2\ \mathbf{2s^2 2p^6}$
Ar $1s^2\ 2s^2 2p^6\ \mathbf{3s^2\ 3p^6}$
Kr $1s^2\ 2s^2 2p^6 3s^2 3p^6 3d^{10}\mathbf{4s^2 4p^6}$
Xe $1s^2\ 2s^2 2p^6 3s^2 3p^6 3d^{10}4s^2 4p^6 4d^{10}\mathbf{5s^2 5p^6}$

Since the atoms of the noble gases were not known to form chemical bonds, it was argued that the presence of 8 electrons (an electron octet) in the valence shell makes the atom stable. Therefore *all other atoms must undergo bonding by gaining or losing or sharing electrons so as to acquire the electronic configuration of the nearest inert gas.* The presence of 8 electrons gives the name **octet rule** to this concept. In the case of the first few elements such as hydrogen, lithium and beryllium the atoms combine in such a way as to attain the stable structure of helium with

2 electrons **(duplet)** in its only one valence shell. There are, however, many exceptions to the octet rule. Also compounds of noble gases, especially xenon, have been synthesized. The various types of chemical bonds are discussed below.

2 | IONIC BOND (OR ELECTROVALENT LINKAGE)

An ionic bond is formed *by the complete transfer of electron(s) from one atom to another.* Atoms of metals generally lose electrons and those of non-metals gain electrons.

(i) Formation of sodium chloride, NaCl

A sodium atom (Z = 11) transfers its valence electron to a chlorine atom (Z = 17). The sodium atom by losing an electron acquires the electronic configuration of neon ($1s^2 2s^2 2p^6$) and becomes sodium ion Na^+ carrying a unit positive charge. The chlorine atom by gaining an electron acquires the stable configuration of argon ($1s^2 2s^2 2p^6 3s^2 3p^6$) and becomes a chloride ion, Cl^-, with a unit negative charge.

The transfer of electron results in the formation of the ionic bond.

$$Na\cdot\ +\ \cdot\ddot{\underset{..}{Cl}}:\ \longrightarrow\ Na^+\ +\ \left[:\ddot{\underset{..}{Cl}}:\right]^-$$

$[Ne]3s^1$ $[Ne]3s^2 3p^5$ $[Ne]$ $[Ar]$

- Here we have used **Lewis dot symbols** in which the symbol of an element is surrounded by dots (or crosses) to represent electrons in the outermost (valence) shell. Formulae of compounds using Lewis symbols are called **Lewis formulae.**

- When atoms form a bond by electron transfer, the **number of electrons lost and gained must be equal,** because the resulting ionic compound is neutral.
- The number of electrons lost or gained by an atom in the formation of an ionic bond is its valence. Thus Na and Cl have a valence of 1.
- **Loss of electron** is called **oxidation;** thus Na is oxidised to Na^+. The **gain of electron is reduction**; thus Cl is reduced to Cl^-. Formation of an ionic bond from elements is an oxidation - reduction or **redox reaction.** Generally the metal is oxidised and the non-metal is reduced.
- Na^+ and Ne are **isoelectronic:** since they contain the **same number of electrons.** Similarly Cl^- and Ar are isoelectronic.
- Because Na^+ and Cl^- carry opposite charges, electrostatic forces of attraction hold them together. Sodium chloride may be represented as Na^+Cl^-.

(ii) Formation of magnesium oxide, MgO

$$Mg: \quad + \quad \ddot{O}: \quad \longrightarrow \quad Mg^{2+} \quad + \quad \left[:\ddot{O}:\right]^{2-}$$

$$[Ne]3s^2 \quad [He]2s^22p^4 \qquad\qquad [Ne] \qquad\qquad [Ne]$$

2.1   CONDITIONS FOR THE FORMATION OF IONIC BOND

(i)   The difference between the electronegativity of two combining atoms must be greater than two.

(ii) **Low ionization energy of the metal:** Low ionization energy means that the metal atom requires only a small amount of energy to release its valence electron. For example, sodium, which has a low I.E. readily gives up its loosely held electron and forms Na^+ ion. Metals of s-block have low ionization energies and so readily form the corresponding cations.

☛ Ionization energy of an element with a single electron in its valence shell is less than that with two electrons. In going across a period of the periodic table from left to right, I.E. increases and the formation of the cation is less likely. On going down a group, the outermost electron gets further away from the nucleus, and hence is more easily removed i.e., I.E. decreases; the formation of the cation becomes more likely.

(iii) **High electron affinity of the non-metal:** An atom with a high electron affinity releases a lot of energy when it takes up an electron and forms an anion. For example, chlorine which has a high electron affinity, readily takes up an electron from the Na atom and forms Cl^- ion. Non-metals of groups VI A and VII A have high electron affinity and can form ionic bonds.

☛ In going across a period from left to right, electron affinity (energy released) increases and so the formation of the negative ion becomes more likely. On going down a group, electron affinity decreases and so the formation of anion becomes less likely.

(iv) **High lattice energy of the crystal:** In the formation of sodium chloride crystal, the Na^+ ion attracts the Cl^- ion to form an ion-pair Na^+Cl^-. Since the electrostatic force of attraction is present in all directions, this ion-pair will attract other ion-pairs and build up into a crystal lattice. A crystal lattice is three dimensional basic pattern of points, in which each point corresponds to a unit of the crystal, say an ion (atom or molecule). As the lattice builds up, energy is released. The energy released when sufficient number of cations and anions come together to form 1 mole of the compound is called the lattice energy of the compound.

Therefore, an ionic compound is formed when the energy released in (iii) and (iv) exceeds the energy absorbed in (ii).

2.2   GENERAL CHARACTERISTICS OF IONIC COMPOUNDS

(i) Generally ionic compounds are hard solids. As single ions of a metal are not associated in the solid with single ions of a non-metal, separate units of ionic compounds do not exist.

It is, therefore, wrong to talk of a molecule of an ionic compound. The formula only indicates the ratio of number of ions and the crystal consists of a very large number of oppositely charged ions. Thus in NaCl crystal each Na^+ ion is surrounded by $6Cl^-$ ions and vice versa (in an octahedral arrangement). The attraction between Na^+ and Cl^- ions is quite large.

(ii) As a good deal of thermal energy is required to overcome the large electrostatic forces of attraction in an ionic crystal, ionic compounds have high melting and boiling points.

(iii) Ionic compounds are commonly soluble in water and other polar solvents (which separate the ions). They are practically insoluble in organic solvents such as benzene, carbon tetrachloride, etc., as there is no attraction between ions and the molecules of the non-polar liquids.

(iv) Ionic compounds are electrolytes. In the presence of an ionizing solvent such as water, the electrostatic forces between the ions are so greatly reduced that the ions get separated. (This is due to the electrostatic attraction between the ions and the polar molecules of the solvent.) The free ions in solution conduct electricity and on passing a current, the ionic compound undergoes chemical decomposition (called electrolysis). When an ionic compound is melted, the crystal lattice structure is broken and free ions are produced. It is the free movement of ions, which makes an ionic compound a conductor and to undergo electrolysis in the molten condition.

(v) When an ionic compound dissolves in water, the ions get solvated (in this case hydrated). The energy released is called solvation energy. This energy counters wholly or in part the high lattice energy of the ionic compound. Insoluble ionic compounds (eg., sulphates, phosphates and fluorides of Ca, Sr and Ba) have very high lattice energies and the solvation energy of the constituent ions is insufficient to counteract the high lattice energies and make them soluble.

(vi) The chemical properties of an ionic compound are the properties of its constituent ions. Thus all chlorides give the characteristic reactions of the chloride ion (reactions with conc. H_2SO_4, $AgNO_3$ solution, etc). All acids, which contain H^+ ions give the same reactions (change blue litmus to red, effervesce with a carbonate, etc).

(vii) Reactions between solutions of ionic compounds are almost instantaneous, because they are reactions between ions (and do not involve the breaking up of bonds as in covalent compounds, q.v.). For example, when silver nitrate solution is added to sodium chloride solution, silver chloride is immediately precipitated. The reaction may be represented thus:

$$Na^+ + Cl^- + Ag^+\, NO_3^- \longrightarrow AgCl + Na^+ + NO_3^-$$

3   COVALENT BOND

A covalent bond is formed by ***the sharing of a pair of electrons between two atoms, each atom contributing one electron to the shared pair***. The shared pair of electrons should have opposite spins and they are localized between the two nuclei concerned. A covalent bond is usually represented by a short line (i.e., a dash) between the two atoms. Note that the covalent bond consists of a pair of electrons shared between two atoms, and occupying a combination of two stable orbitals, one of each atom; the shared electrons of each covalent bond are counted for each of the two atoms connected by the covalent bond. The difference between the electronegativities of the combining atoms is less than two.

(1)   **Formation of the hydrogen molecule**

Each hydrogen atom requires 1 electron to become isoelectronic with helium, the nearest inert gas. The hydrogen atoms share their electrons thus:

$$H\cdot \quad + \quad \cdot H \quad \longrightarrow \quad H\!\cdot\!\cdot\!H \ \text{ or } \ H\text{–}H$$

Once the covalent bond is formed, the two bonding electrons are attracted by the two nuclei (instead of one) and the bonded state is more stable than the non-bonded state. The resultant attraction is responsible for the strength of the covalent bond.

(2) Formation of hydrogen fluoride

The hydrogen atom has in its orbital 1 electron. It can achieve the helium configuration by forming a single covalent bond with another atom. Fluorine has 7 electrons in its outer, i.e., L shell. F can acquire the Neon configuration by forming a single covalent bond using its unpaired electron. This may be represented as follows.

$$H\cdot + \cdot \ddot{\underset{..}{F}}: \longrightarrow H:\ddot{\underset{..}{F}}: \quad \text{or} \quad H-F$$

The single covalent bond holds the H and F atoms firmly together. Similarly we can explain the formation of HCl, HBr and HI.

(3) Formation of water, H_2O

$$:\ddot{\underset{..}{O}}: + 2H \longrightarrow :\ddot{\underset{..}{O}}:H \quad \text{or} \quad \overset{\displaystyle H}{\underset{\displaystyle }{:\underset{..}{O}-H}}$$

Similarly we can explain the formation of H_2S (hydrogen sulphide), H_2Se (hydrogen selenide) and H_2Te (hydrogen telluride).

(4) Formation of ammonia, NH_3

$$\cdot\ddot{N} + 3H \longrightarrow \underset{\displaystyle H}{H:\ddot{N}:H} \quad \text{or} \quad \underset{\displaystyle H}{H-\ddot{N}-H}$$

The structures of phosphine (PH_3), arsine (AsH_3) and stibine (SbH_3) are similar to that of ammonia.

(5) Formation of carbon tetrachloride, CCl_4

$$\cdot\dot{C}\cdot + 4\ \cdot\ddot{Cl}: \longrightarrow \underset{\displaystyle :\ddot{Cl}:}{\overset{\displaystyle :\ddot{Cl}:}{:\ddot{Cl}:\ C\ :\ddot{Cl}:}} \quad \text{or} \quad \underset{\displaystyle Cl}{\overset{\displaystyle Cl}{Cl-C-Cl}}$$

(6) Formation of methane, CH_4

$$\cdot\dot{C}\cdot + 4H \longrightarrow \underset{\displaystyle H}{\overset{\displaystyle H}{H:C:H}} \quad \text{or} \quad \underset{\displaystyle H}{\overset{\displaystyle H}{H-C-H}}$$

(7) Formation of ethane, C_2H_6

$$2\cdot\dot{C}\cdot + 6H \longrightarrow \underset{\displaystyle H\ H}{\overset{\displaystyle H\ H}{H:C:C:H}} \quad \text{or} \quad \underset{\displaystyle H\ H}{\overset{\displaystyle H\ H}{H-C-C-H.}}$$

☛ **(i)** The number of electrons needed by an atom to acquire its octet (C-4, N-3, O-2, Cl-1) is equal to the number of covalent bonds commonly formed.

(ii) When two pairs of electrons are shared between two atoms, there is a double bond as in ethylene, C_2H_4.

$$\underset{\displaystyle H}{\overset{\displaystyle H}{}}\ C::C\ \underset{\displaystyle H}{\overset{\displaystyle H}{}} \qquad \underset{\displaystyle H}{\overset{\displaystyle H}{}}C=C\underset{\displaystyle H}{\overset{\displaystyle H}{}}$$

(iii) When three pairs of electrons are shared between two atoms, there is a triple bond as in acetylene, C_2H_2.

$$H \cdot \cdot C \vdots C \cdot \cdot H \quad \text{or} \quad H-C \equiv C-H$$

(iv) Generally all atoms involved in covalent bonding have completed octets (except hydrogen, which has a duplet of electrons). Sometimes an atom forms more than 4 covalent bonds.

An example is phosphorus pentachloride PCl_5. In this molecule phosphorus atom is surrounded by 5 chlorine atoms, with each of which it forms a covalent bond (with some ionic character, about which we shall learn later). In this compound the phosphorus atom seems to use 5 of the nine orbitals of the M shell (rather than only 4 of the most stable orbitals). It seems likely that of the nine or more orbitals in the M, N and O shells, four are especially stable, but one or more others may be occasionally utilized.

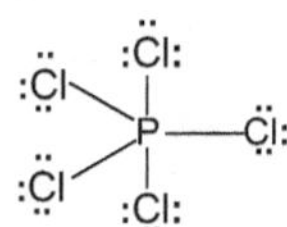

Another example is SF_6

3.1 GENERAL CHARACTERISTICS OF COVALENT COMPOUNDS

(i) In a purely covalent compound the electrons in the bond are shared equally between the atoms linked by the bond; the resultant particles formed are not electrically charged. So, separate molecules of the covalent compounds exist. Covalent compounds may therefore be expected to be gases or low boiling liquids or soft, low melting solids at ordinary temperature. In the solid state they may be amorphous or present as molecular crystals, the molecules being held together by what are called weak van der Waals' forces of attraction.

(ii) Since the molecules are held together by weak van der Waals' forces, covalent compounds (except those consisting of giant molecules) have low melting and boiling points; very little thermal energy is needed to overcome these weak intermolecular forces.

(iii) They are non-electrolytes, i.e., they do not contain ions. Even in giant molecules such as diamond there are no free electrons. So they are very poor conductors of electricity.

(iv) They are generally soluble in organic (non-polar) solvents such as benzene or carbon tetrachloride but are insoluble in water or other ionizing solvents. (The solubility of covalent compounds is very much dependent on the size of the molecules; giant molecules are practically insoluble in nearly all solvents.)

(v) Reactions between covalent compounds are slow and often incomplete and reversible. This is so because the reaction involves breaking and making of bonds i.e., energy considerations are involved for reactants, activated complexes and products.

(vi) A covalent bond is a space-directed bond and it may exhibit isomerism.

3.2 POLAR COVALENT BONDS – ELECTRONEGATIVITY

The shared pair of electrons may be shared equally between two atoms; then the covalent bond is said to be non-polar. Equal sharing occurs between identical atoms, as in H – H or Cl – Cl (i.e., in homonuclear molecules) or between identical atoms with identical neighbours as in $H_3C–CH_3$. When the two bonded atoms are dissimilar (i.e., in heteronuclear molecules) the sharing is unequal. For example a chlorine atom has a greater electron attracting power than a hydrogen atom; so in H – Cl, the shared pair of electrons are drawn more towards chlorine and away from hydrogen. The result is separation of charges within the molecule, the chlorine end acquiring a slight negative charge and the hydrogen end a slight but equal positive charge: $\overset{\delta+}{H}\!\!-\!\!-\!\!-\!\!\overset{\delta-}{Cl}$. Such covalent bonds are said to be polar (i.e., bonds formed by sharing a pair of electrons between two atoms but displaced towards the nucleus of one of the bonded atoms).

The net tendency of a bonded atom in a covalent molecule to attract the shared pair of electrons towards itself is known as electronegativity. (This word does not mean the actual content of the electric charge, but just the tendency to acquire it in a molecule). Thus F is highly electronegative, but F⁻, which has already an extra electron, is not.

Table 3.2a: Table of Electronegativities (Pauling)

H 2.1						
Li 1.0	Be 1.5	B 2.0	C 2.5	N 3.0	O 3.5	F 4.0
Na 0.9	Mg 1.2	Al 1.5	Si 1.8	P 2.1	S 2.5	Cl 3.0
K 0.8	Ca 1.0			As 2.0	Se 2.4	Br 2.8
Rb 0.8	Sr 1.0			Sb 1.9	Te 2.1	I 2.5

To assess the tendency of an atom of a given element to attract electrons towards itself in a covalent bond, relative electronegativity values are used. Table 3.2a. gives the relative electronegativity values of atoms calculated by Pauling (adopting arbitrarily the value of 4 units for the electronegativity of fluorine).

- **(i)** Electronegativity values increase across a period and decrease down a group.
- **(ii)** Smaller atoms have greater electronegativity than larger ones and so they attract electrons more towards them than larger ones. Alkali metals have low electronegativities and halogens high electronegativities.
- **(iii)** Atoms with nearly filled shells of electrons (e.g., halogens) have greater electronegativity than those with sparsely occupied shells.
- **(iv)** Elements with low electronegativity values such as Cs (0.8) and Rb (0.8) tend to form positive ions, i.e., these are metals. Elements with high electronegativity values such as F(4.0) and O(3.5) tend to form negative ions, i.e., these are non-metals.
- **(v)** Electronegativity value may be used to make rough predictions of the type of bonding to be found in a compound. The larger the difference between electronegativity values of two combining atoms, the more polar the covalent bond. If the difference is greater than 2, the greater the chance for ionic bonding (i.e., the chance of covalent bond assuming 100% ionic character). From this point of view ionic bond may be considered to be an extreme case of a polar bond (with total separation of charges).

  If the difference between the electronegativities of the combining atoms is zero or small, the bond is essentially non-polar.

  Let X_A and X_B represent the electronegativities of two atoms A and B.

  If $X_B - X_A = 1.7$, the covalent bond A – B is said to have 50% ionic character. On this basis, the % ionic character in some typical bonds is calculated (Table 3.2b). These calculations are very qualitative.

Table 3.2b: % Ionic Character of Bonds

C – H	N – H	O – H	F – H
4%	19%	39%	60%
C – F	C – Cl	C – Br	C – I
43%	11%	3%	0%

3.3 DIPOLE MOMENTS

A dipole consists of a positive and an equal negative charge separated by a distance within a molecule. The degree of polarity of a bond is given by the dipole moment (μ), which is the product of either charge (e) and the distance (d) between them. $\mu = d \times e$. 'e' is of the order of magnitude of the electronic charge, i.e., about 10^{-10} esu and d is the distance between the atomic centres, i.e., about 10^{-8} cm. Hence dipole moments may be expected to have values around $10^{-10} \times 10^{-8} = 10^{-18}$ esu-cm. It is however, general practice to express dipole moments in **Debye units** (D), $1\,D = 10^{-18}$ esu-cm.

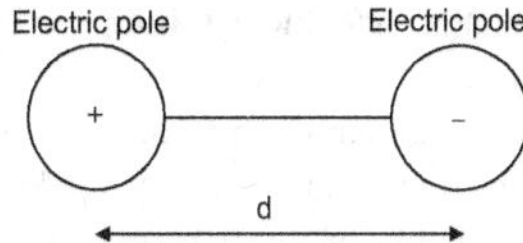

If the charge is in SI units (Coulombs) and d in metre, μ will be coulomb-metre (C ·m) units. $1D = 3.336 \times 10^{-30}$ C · m.

Any covalent bond which has a certain degree of polarity will have a corresponding dipole moment, though it does not follow that compounds containing such bonds will have dipole moments, for the *polarity of the molecule as a whole is the vector sum of the individual bond moments*. For example, CO_2 has zero dipole moment, although the $C = O$ bond is a polar bond. This shows that CO_2 is a linear molecule, $O = C = O$, so that the dipole moments of the two $C = O$ bonds cancel out. The $C \rightarrow Cl$ bond has a definite polarity and a definite dipole moment but carbon tetrachloride has zero dipole moment because it is a tetrahedral molecule, and the resultant of the $4C - Cl$ bond moments is zero. On the contrary CH_3Cl, CH_2Cl_2 and $CHCl_3$ have definite dipole moments.

3.4 APPLICATIONS OF DIPOLE MOMENT MEASUREMENTS

Dipole moment is a measure of the electrical dissymmetry (polarity) in the molecule and so its measurement provides valuable information concerning the shapes of molecules. Conversely, when the symmetry of the molecules is known, dipole moment could be estimated fairly.

(A) Inorganic substances:

(i) **Monatomic molecules** such as He, Ne, etc., have zero dipole moment because they are symmetrical.

(ii) **Diatomic molecules** such as H_2, Cl_2 and N_2 have no dipole moment; so these molecules are symmetrical.

(iii) **Triatomic molecules:** Some of these molecules possess zero dipole moment; so they have a symmetrical linear structure, e.g., CO_2, CS_2, $HgCl_2$. Others like water and sulphur dioxide have definite dipole moments. They are said to have angular or bent structure or V-shaped structure.

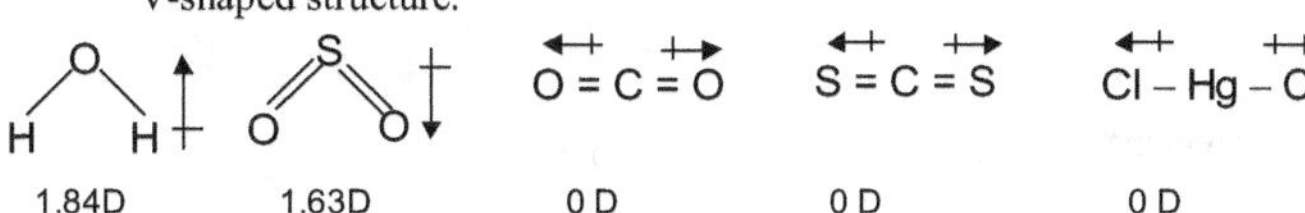

(iv) Tetratomic molecules: Some molecules like BCl_3 have zero dipole moment. They are said to possess a flat and symmetrical (triangular) structure; other examples are BF_3, BBr_3, CO_3^{2-} and NO_3^-.

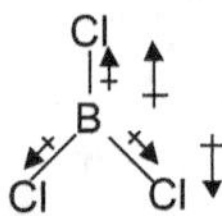

PCl_3, $AsCl_3$, NH_3, PH_3, AsH_3, H_3O^+ have appreciable dipole moments. They possess trigonal pyramidal structures.

Illustration 1

Question: **Both CO_2 and N_2O are linear but dipole moment of CO_2 in zero but for N_2O it is non–zero, why?**

Solution: The answer lies in the structure of these molecules. CO_2 is a symmetrical molecule while N_2O is unsymmetrical. Thus for N_2O, dipoles do not cancel each other, leaving the molecule with a resultant dipole, while the bond moment of CO_2 cancel each other, so CO_2 has no net dipole moment.

$$N \equiv N \rightarrow O \quad ; \quad O = C = O$$

Illustration 2

Question: **Compare the dipole moment of NH_3 and NF_3.**

Solution: Let's draw the structure of both the compounds and then analyse their dipole directions.

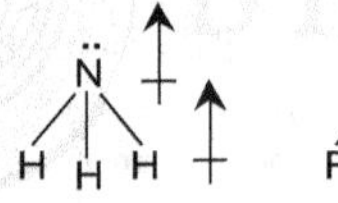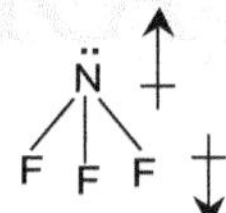

The structure of both NH_3 and NF_3 are pyramidal with three bond pairs and one lone pair. In NH_3, as N is more electronegative than hydrogen, so the resultant bond dipole is towards N, which means that both the lone pair and bond pair dipoles are acting in the same direction and are summed up. In case of NF_3, the bond dipole (of N–F bonds) is acting towards fluorine, (as fluorine is more electronegative than N) so in NF_3 the lone pair and bond pair dipoles are acting in opposition, resulting in a decreased dipole moment. Thus, NH_3 has higher dipole moment than NF_3.

(B) Organic substances

(i) Methane and CCl_4 have zero dipole moment. So they possess symmetrical tetrahedral structures with C atom at the centre of the tetrahedron.

Methane

(ii) **Benzene** has zero dipole moment. All the 6 C and 6 H atoms are assumed to be in the same plane (symmetrical hexagonal structure).

(iii) **Measurement of dipole moments will enable** us to detect cis-and trans–isomers of organic compounds (you will learn about cis–trans or geometrical isomerism later in the organic chemistry). The trans– isomer, which is symmetrical, has zero dipole moment while the cis–isomer has a definite dipole moment.

cis-dibromoethylene ($\mu = 1.4$ D)   trans-dibromoethylene ($\mu = 0$)

(iv) **Dipole moment in aromatic ring system**

The dipole moments of the aromatic compounds present a very good illustration of dipole moment. We know that when substituted benzene is treated with reagent different products (namely ortho, meta and para products) are formed. The dipole moments of these products are different since the orientation of the groups is different. Let us take an example to clarify it. Let us take three isomers, o–nitrophenol, m–nitrophenol and p–nitrophenol. We have also have three other isomers, o–aminophenol, m–aminophenol and p–aminophenol. We want to arrange these isomers in the order of their dipole moments.

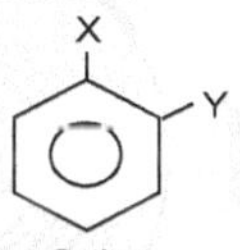

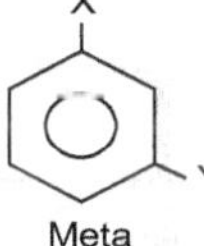

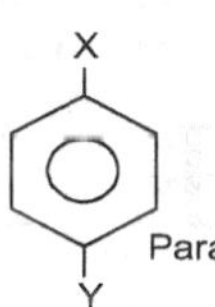

In those cases where X = Y, the para isomer becomes symmetrical and have zero dipole moment. In order to find their dipole moment, we need to know about the nature of the groups linked to the benzene ring. In nitro phenols, one group (OH) is electron pushing and the other (NO_2) is electron withdrawing while in aminophenols, both the groups (OH and NH_2) attached are electron pushing. So, depending on the nature of the groups attached, the isomers have different dipole moment. Then calculation of dipole moment follows as:

Case (i): When X and Y both are electron pushing or electron withdrawing.

Let the bond dipole of C–X bond is represented by μ_1 and that of C–Y bond by μ_2. Now let us assume that the electron pushing groups have +ve bond moment and the electron withdrawing groups have –ve bond moment. The net dipole moment is the resultant of two bond dipoles at different orientations.

$$\mu_{ortho} = \sqrt{\mu_1^2 + \mu_2^2 + 2\mu_1\mu_2\cos 60^\circ} = \sqrt{\mu_1^2 + \mu_2^2 + 2\mu_1\mu_2 \cdot \frac{1}{2}}$$

$$\therefore\ \mu_0 = \sqrt{\mu_1^2 + \mu_2^2 + \mu_1\mu_2}$$

$$\mu_{meta} = \sqrt{\mu_1^2 + \mu_2^2 + 2\mu_1\mu_2\cos 120^\circ}$$

$$\therefore\ \mu_m = \sqrt{\mu_1^2 + \mu_2^2 - \mu_1\mu_2}$$

$$\mu_{para} = \sqrt{\mu_1^2 + \mu_2^2 + 2\mu_1\mu_2\cos 180^\circ} = \sqrt{\mu_1^2 + \mu_2^2 - 2\mu_1\mu_2}$$

$$\therefore\ \mu_p = \mu_1 - \mu_2$$

From the above expressions of μ_0, μ_m and μ_p, it is clear that when both X and Y are of the same nature i.e., both are electron withdrawing or both are electron pushing the para product has the least dipole moment and ortho product has the highest dipole moment. When X = Y, $\mu_1 = \mu_2$, thus μ_p would be zero.

Case (ii): When X is electron pushing and Y is electron withdrawing or vice versa.

Let the bond moment of C–X dipole is μ_1 and that of C–Y dipole is μ_2.

$$\mu_0 = \sqrt{\mu_1^2 + (-\mu_2)^2 + 2\mu_1(-\mu_2)\cos 60°}$$

$$= \sqrt{\mu_1^2 + \mu_2^2 - \mu_1\mu_2}$$

$$= \sqrt{(\mu_1 + \mu_2)^2 - 3\mu_1\mu_2}$$

$$\mu_{meta} = \sqrt{\mu_1^2 + (-\mu_2)^2 + 2\mu_1(-\mu_2)\cos 120°}$$

$$= \sqrt{\mu_1^2 + \mu_2^2 + \mu_1\mu_2}$$

$$= \sqrt{(\mu_1 + \mu_2)^2 - \mu_1\mu_2}$$

$$\mu_{para} = \sqrt{\mu_1^2 + (-\mu_2)^2 + 2\mu_1(-\mu_2)\cos 180°}$$

$$= \sqrt{\mu_1^2 + \mu_2^2 + 2\mu_1\mu_2} = \mu_1 + \mu_2$$

Looking at the expressions of μ_0, μ_m and μ_p, it is clear that the para isomer has the highest dipole moment and ortho has the least.

3.5   DIPOLE MOMENT AND PERCENTAGE IONIC CHARACTER

The measured dipole moment of a substance may be used to calculate the percentage ionic character of a covalent bond in simple molecules.

1 unit charge = Magnitude of electronic charge = 4.8×10^{-10} e.s.u.

$1\ D = 1 \times 10^{-18}$ e.s.u–cm.

$$\therefore \% \text{ ionic character} = \frac{\text{Observed dipole moment}}{\text{Theoretical dipole moment}} \times 100$$

Theoretical dipole moment is confined to when we assume that the bond is 100 % ionic and it is broken into ions while observed dipole moment is with respect to fractional charges on the atoms of the bond.

3.6   TRANSITION FROM IONIC TO COVALENT BOND – FAJANS' RULE

Just as a covalent bond may have partial ionic character, an ionic bond may also show a certain degree of covalent character. When two oppositely charged ions approach each other closely, the cation would attract the electrons in the outer shell of the anion and simultaneously repel its nucleus. This produces distortion or polarization of the anion, which is accompanied by some sharing of electrons between the ions, i.e., the bond acquires a certain covalent character. The formation of a covalent bond between two ions may be illustrated with reference to formation of AgI.

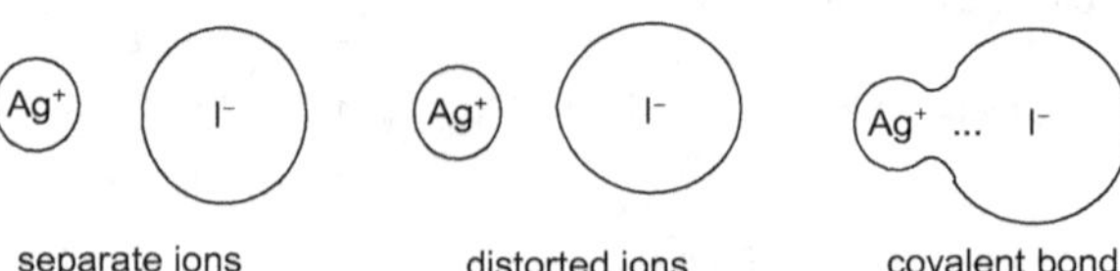

| separate ions | distorted ions | covalent bond |

FACTORS INFLUENCING ION – DEFORMATION OR INCREASING COVALENT CHARACTER

(i) Large charge on the ions:

The greater the charge on the cation, the more strongly will it attract the electrons of the anion. For example, Al^{3+} can distort Cl^- ion more than Na^+ ion. So aluminium chloride is a covalent compound whereas NaCl, AlF_3 , AgF are ionic.

(ii) Small cation and large anion:

For a small cation, the electrostatic force with which its nucleus will attract the anion will be large. Moreover a large anion cannot hold the electrons in its outermost shell, especially when they are attracted by a neighbouring cation. Hence there will be increased covalence with a small cation and a large anion, as in AgI.

(iii) Cation with a non-inert gas type of electronic configuration:

A cation with a 18 electron outermost shell such as Ag^+ ([Kr] $4d^{10}$) polarizes anions more strongly than a cation with a 8 electron arrangement as in K^+. The 'd' electrons in Ag^+ do not screen the nuclear charge as effectively as the 's' and 'p' electron shell in K^+. Thus AgI is more covalent than KI, although Ag^+ and K^+ ions are nearly of the same size. Cuprous and mercurous salts are covalent. The above statements regarding the factors, which influence covalent character, are called Fajans' rules. It can thus be seen easily that there is nothing like a purely ionic compound or a purely covalent compound.

4 LEWIS STRUCTURES OF MOLECULES

The formula of a molecule shows the number of atoms of each element but does not show the bonding arrangement of the atoms. To represent the bonding pattern in a molecule, the electron dot symbols of the elements are arranged such that the shared pairs and unshared pairs (called lone pairs) are shown and the octet rule (or duet for hydrogen) is satisfied. For example,

a molecule of fluorine is shown as : $\ddot{F}$: $\ddot{F}$: or : $\ddot{F}$ ——$\ddot{F}$: and a molecule of hydrogen fluoride is shown as

H : $\ddot{F}$:   or   H——$\ddot{F}$: .

Arrangement of dot symbols used to represent molecules are called **Lewis structures**. Lewis structures do not convey any information regarding the shape of the molecule. Usually, the shared pairs of electrons are represented by lines between atoms and any unshared pairs are shown as dot pairs.

Lewis structures are written by fitting the element dot symbols together to show shared electron pairs and to satisfy the octet rule. For example,

(i)   In water (H_2O), one $\dot{H}$ and two $\cdot \ddot{O}$: complete their duet and octet respectively as

: $\ddot{O}$——H
|
H

(ii)   In ammonia (NH_3), three $\dot{H}$ and one $\cdot \ddot{N} \cdot$ fit together and satisfy their duet and octet

respectively as   H——$\ddot{N}$——H
|
H

(iii)   In carbon tetrachloride (CCl_4), four : $\ddot{Cl} \cdot$ and one $\cdot \dot{C} \cdot$ complete their octet as

:$\ddot{Cl}$:
|
:$\ddot{Cl}$——C——$\ddot{Cl}$:
|
:$\ddot{Cl}$:

For the given molecules, we have adopted hit & trial method to fit the dot symbols together and satisfy the octet rule. But remember that hydrogen form one bond, oxygen forms two bonds, nitrogen three bonds and carbon forms four bonds. For simpler molecules, the hit & trial method works perfectly but for slightly complicated polyatomic species, this may give us more than one possible structure. Thus, a systematic approach is needed to design the Lewis structures of such polyatomic species. But before proceeding further, let us understand the limitation of this approach.

4.1   LIMITATIONS OF LEWIS THEORY OF DRAWING STRUCTURE

This method would be applicable to only those molecules/species, which follow octet rule except hydrogen.

There are three kinds of molecules/species, which do not follow octet rule.

(a)   Molecules, which have contraction of octet. Such molecules are electron deficient. For example, BH_3, BF_3, BCl_3, $AlCl_3$, $GaCl_3$ etc.

(b)   Molecules, which have expansion of octet. Such species have more than eight electrons in their outermost shell. This is possible in those molecules, which have vacant d–orbitals, thus they can expand their octet. For example, PCl_5, SF_6 etc.

(c)   Molecules containing odd number of electrons (in total) cannot satisfy octet rule. Such species are called odd electron species and are paramagnetic in nature due to presence of unpaired electron. For example, NO, NO_2 and ClO_2.

4.2   METHOD OF DRAWING LEWIS STRCUTURES

To draw the Lewis structures of polyatomic species, follow the given sequence.

(i)   First calculate n_1.

n_1 = Sum of valence electron of all the atoms of the species ± net charge on the species. For a negatively charged species, electrons are added while for positively charged species, the electrons are subtracted. For an uninegatively charged species, add 1 to the sum of valence electrons and for a dinegatively charged species, add 2 and so on.

(ii)   Then calculate n_2.

$n_2 = (8 \times$ number of atoms other than H) + $(2 \times$ number of H atoms)

(iii)   Subtract n_1 from n_2, which gives n_3.

$n_3 = n_2 - n_1$ = number of electrons shared between atoms = number of bonding electrons.

$$\frac{n_3}{2} = \frac{n_2 - n_1}{2} = \text{number of shared (bonding) electron pairs} = \text{number of bonds.}$$

(iv)   Subtracting n_3 from n_1 gives n_4.

$n_4 = n_1 - n_3$ = number of unshared electrons or non–bonding electrons.

$$\frac{n_4}{2} = \frac{n_1 - n_3}{2} = \text{number of unshared electron pairs} = \text{number of lone pairs.}$$

(v)   Identify the central atom. Generally, the central atom is the one, which is least electronegative of all the atoms, when the other atoms do not contain hydrogen. When the other atoms are hydrogen only, then the central atom would be the more electronegative atom. However some exceptions are possible, for example Cl_2O.

(vi)   Now around the central atom, place the other atoms and distribute the required number of bonds (as calculated in step (iii)) & required number of lone pairs (as calculated in step (iv)), keeping in mind that every atom gets an octet of electrons except hydrogen.

(vii)   Then calculate the formal charge on each atom of the species.

Formal charge on an atom = number of valence electrons of the atom – number of bonds formed by that atom – number of unshared electrons (2 × lone pairs) of that atom.

(viii) When two adjacent atoms get opposite formal charges, then charges can be removed by replacing the covalent bond between the atoms by a dative (co–ordinate) bond. This bond will have the arrowhead pointing towards the atom with negative formal charge. It is not mandatory to show the dative bonds unless required to do so.

(ix) The given Lewis structure should account for the factual aspects of the molecule like resonance (delocalization), bond length, $p\pi$–$d\pi$ back bonding etc.
Sometimes, there are more than one acceptable Lewis structure for a given species. In such cases, we select the most plausible Lewis structure by using formal charges and the following guidelines:

- For neutral molecules, a Lewis structure in which there are no formal charges is preferable to one in which formal charges are present.

- Lewis structures with large formal charges (+2, +3 and/ or –2, –3 and so on) are less plausible than those with small formal charges.

- Among Lewis structures having similar distributions of formal charges, the most plausible structure is the one in which negative formal charges are placed on the more electronegative atoms.

Illustration 3

Question: **Determine Lewis structure of NO_3^- ion.**

Solution:

(i) $n_1 = 5 + (6 \times 3) + 1 = 24$

(ii) $n_2 = (4 \times 8) = 32$

(iii) $n_3 = n_2 - n_1 = 32 - 24 = 8$

$$\therefore \text{Number of bonds} = \frac{8}{2} = 4$$

(iv) $n_4 = n_1 - n_3 = 24 - 8 = 16$

$$\therefore \text{Number of lone pairs} = \frac{16}{2} = 8$$

(v) Nitrogen is the central atom (as it is less electronegative than O). Arranging three O atoms around it and distributing 4 bonds and 8 lone pairs as

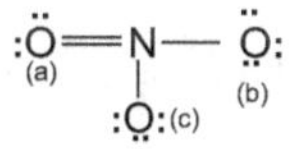

$$:\!\ddot{O}\!\!=\!\!N\!\!-\!\!\ddot{O}\!: \quad \big| \quad :\!\ddot{O}\!:$$

(vi) Calculating formal change on each atom.

Formal charge on N = $5 - 4 - 0 = +1$

Formal charge on O (a) = $6 - 2 - 4 = 0$

Formal charge on O (b) = $6 - 1 - 6 = -1$

Formal charge on O (c) = $6 - 1 - 6 = -1$

Thus, the structures can now be shown as

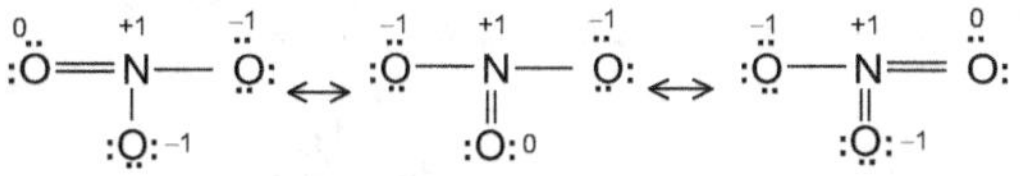

$$:\!\ddot{O}\!\!=\!\!N\!\!-\!\!\ddot{O}\!: \;\longleftrightarrow\; :\!\ddot{O}\!\!-\!\!N\!\!-\!\!\ddot{O}\!: \;\longleftrightarrow\; :\!\ddot{O}\!\!-\!\!N\!\!=\!\!\ddot{O}\!:$$

Final structure of NO_3^- is therefore shown as

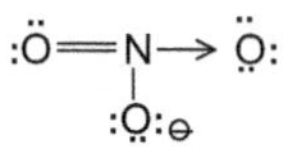

$$:\!\ddot{O}\!\!=\!\!N\!\!\longrightarrow\!\ddot{O}\!: \quad \big| \quad :\!\ddot{O}\!:^{\ominus}$$

which even accounts for resonance in NO_3^- ion.

Illustration 4

Question: Determine Lewis structure of CN^- ion.

Solution:

(i) $n_1 = 4 + 5 + 1 = 10$

(ii) $n_2 = (2 \times 8) = 16$

(iii) $n_3 = n_2 - n_1 = 16 - 10 = 6$

$\therefore$ Number of bonds $= \dfrac{6}{2} = 3$

(iv) $n_4 = n_1 - n_3 = 10 - 6 = 4$

$\therefore$ Number of lone pairs $= \dfrac{4}{2} = 2$

(v)   Carbon is the central atom (C is less electronegative than N) and arrange N, number of bonds and number of lone pairs around it as

$$:C\!\equiv\!N:$$

(vi)   Formal charge on C $= 4 - 3 - 2 = -1$

Formal charge on N $= 5 - 3 - 2 = 0$

Thus, final Lewis structure of CN^- would be

$$:\overset{\ominus}{C}\!\equiv\!N:$$

Illustration 5

Question: Draw Lewis structure for NH_4^+ ion.

Solution:

(i) $n_1 = 5 + (4 \times 1) - 1 = 8$

(ii) $n_2 = (8 \times 1) + (2 \times 4) = 16$

(iii) $n_3 = n_2 - n_1 = 16 - 8 = 8$

$\therefore$ Number of bonds $= \dfrac{8}{2} = 4$

(iv) $n_4 = n_1 - n_3 = 8 - 8 = 0$

$\therefore$ Number of lone pairs $= 0$

(v)   Nitrogen being the central atom, distributing other atoms (H) around it, and 4 bonds with the 4 H atoms, the structure looks like

$$\begin{array}{c}
H_{(b)}\\
|\\
H_{(a)}\!-\!N\!-\!H_{(c)}\\
|\\
H_{(d)}
\end{array}$$

(vi)   Formal charge on N $= 5 - 4 - 0 = +1$

Formal charge on H(a)/H(b)/H(c)/H(d) $= 1 - 1 - 0 = 0$

Thus, final Lewis structure of NH_4^+ would be

$$\begin{array}{c}
H\\
|\\
H\!-\!\overset{\oplus}{N}\!-\!H\\
|\\
H
\end{array}$$

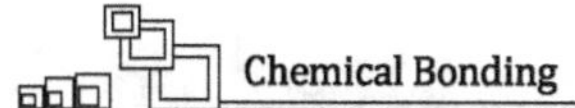

5 | CO-ORDINATE COVALENT BOND OR DATIVE BOND

We have seen that in the formation of a covalent bond between two atoms, each atom contributes one electron to the shared pair. Sometimes *both the electrons of the shared pair may come from one of the atoms. The covalent bond thus formed is a co–ordinate bond or dative bond.*

(i) Formation of ammonium ion

The ammonia molecule has a lone pair of electrons i.e., an unshared pair. The hydrogen ion H^+, has an empty s orbital. The lone pair comes to be shared between the nitrogen and hydrogen atoms:

$$H:\overset{\cdot\cdot}{\underset{H}{N}}: + H^+ \longrightarrow \left[H:\overset{H}{\underset{H}{N}}:H \right] \quad or \quad \left[H-\overset{H}{\underset{H}{N}}\rightarrow H \right]^+$$

Nitrogen atom is called the donor and H^+, the acceptor. The arrow-head in $N \longrightarrow H$ shows that N–atom is electron donor and H–atom is electron acceptor. NH_3 is a neutral molecule. H^+ carries a unit positive charge; so NH_4^+ ion carries a unit positive charge. Once the NH_4^+ ion is formed, all the N–H bonds become identical.

(ii) Hydronium ion, H_3O^+

$$\underset{H \quad H}{\overset{\cdot\cdot}{O}} \quad + \quad H^+ \quad \longrightarrow \quad \underset{H \quad H \quad H}{\overset{\cdot\cdot}{O}}{}^+$$

(iii) Aluminium chloride, Al_2Cl_6

$$\begin{array}{c} Cl \quad \quad Cl \quad \quad Cl \\ \diagdown \quad \diagup \searrow \quad \diagup \\ Al \quad \quad Al \\ \diagup \quad \nwarrow \diagdown \quad \diagdown \\ Cl \quad \quad Cl \quad \quad Cl \end{array}$$

Nitromethane, CH_3NO_2

$$H-\overset{H}{\underset{H}{C}}-N\underset{O}{\overset{O}{\diagup\diagdown}}$$

GENERAL CHARACTERISTICS OF COORDINATE COVALENT COMPOUNDS

As is to be expected the properties of coordinate covalent compounds are mostly similar to the properties of covalent compounds.

(i) The nuclei in coordinate covalent compounds (such as in NH_4^+) are held firmly by shared electrons and so do not form ions in water.

(ii) Their covalent nature makes them sparingly soluble in water and more soluble in organic solvents.

(iii) The coordinate bond is also rigid and directional, just like covalent bonds.

6 | RESONANCE

Carbon dioxide may be represented by Lewis dot formula as

$$:\overset{\cdot\cdot}{O}::C::\overset{\cdot\cdot}{O}: \quad or \quad O=C=O \qquad \qquad \dots (i)$$

The bond length of C O is 1.22 Å, but the actual measured value is 1.15 Å. Further CO_2 is quite stable and does not show the characteristic reactions of the carbonyl group, as shown by aldehydes and ketones. Without shifting, the relative positions of atoms of CO_2 can be represented by two more Lewis formulae:

$$O \equiv C \rightarrow O \qquad\qquad O \leftarrow C \equiv O$$

     (ii)   (iii)

In (ii) and (iii), the two bonds between C and O are different, one being a triple bond and the other a single bond. Both the C–O bonds in CO_2 are identical. It is now obvious that none of these structures actually represents CO_2. To explain this difficulty the concept of resonance was introduced, according to which CO_2 cannot be accurately depicted by any Lewis formula. The actual structure of CO_2 is a resonance hybrid of the three structures:

$$O = C = O \longleftrightarrow O \Rrightarrow C \rightarrow O \longleftrightarrow O \leftarrow C \Lleftarrow O.$$

These different structures are called the ***canonical or contributing structures***. *The actual structure of CO_2 is different from the canonical structures and although it is closely related to them, the actual structure cannot be represented on paper* using the accepted symbols. **All the molecules of CO_2 have the same structure.** Usually, a double–headed arrow $\longleftrightarrow$ is used between the canonical structures.

6.1 CONDITIONS FOR RESONANCE

Resonance can occur when the canonical structures

  (i) have the constituent atoms in the same relative positions;

  (ii) have nearly the same energy;

 (iii) have the same number of unpaired electrons (to allow for continuous change from one type of bond to another);

  (iv) differ in the distribution of electrons around the constituent atoms;

  (v) (molecules or ions) are planar.

6.2 RESONANCE ENERGY

The resonance hybrid is a more stable structure than any of the contributing structures. This means that resonance hybrid has less energy than any of the contributing structures. *The difference in energy between the actual observed energy of the resonance hybrid and the most stable of the contributing structures is called resonance energy.*

For CO_2, structure (i) has less energy than structure (ii).

6.3 OTHER EXAMPLES OF RESONANCE

(i) Sulphur dioxide SO_2

(ii) Nitrous oxide (dinitrogen oxide), N_2O

$$N = N = O \longleftrightarrow N \equiv N \rightarrow O \quad \text{or} \quad N \equiv \overset{+}{N} - \overset{-}{O}$$

(iii) Nitric oxide, NO

$$\ddot{:}\ddot{N} = \ddot{O}: \longleftrightarrow \ddot{:}\ddot{N} = \ddot{O}:$$

(iv) Nitrate ion, NO_3^- (planar, triangular)

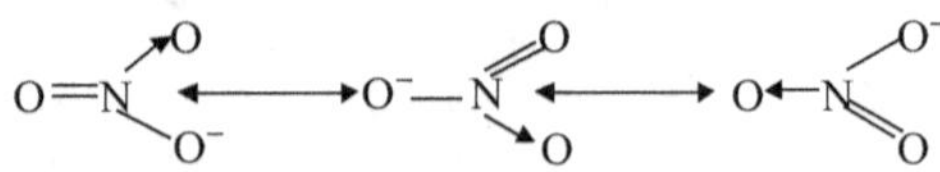

(v) Carbonate ion, CO_3^{2-} (planar, triangular)

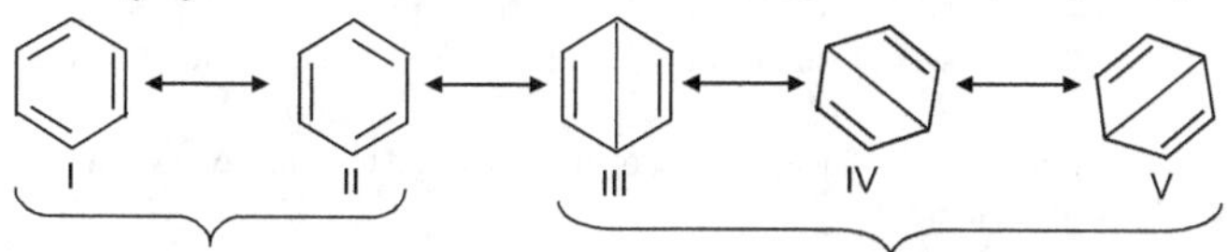

(vi) Benzene, C_6H_6. It is a resonance hybrid of the following structures (hexagonal, planar).

I   II   III   IV   V

Kekule Structures   **Dewar Structures**

C–C bond length is 1.54 Å; C=C bond length is 1.34 Å. In benzene, all the
C–C bonds are identical in length, 1.39 Å, i.e., intermediate between those of single and double
bonds. Note that shortening of bond length and therefore increased stability is an indication of the
existence of resonance [Decrease in dipole moment also indicates resonance]. Resonance energy of
benzene is –152 kJ/mol.

PROFICIENCY TEST– I

The following 10 questions deal with the basic concepts of this section. Answer the following briefly. Go to the next section only if your score is greater than or equal to 8.
Do not consult the study material while attempting the questions.

1. True/False.   Every element tries to acquire the electronic configuration of the nearest noble gas.

2. True/False.   Equal sharing of electrons lead to ionic bond while transfer of electrons lead to covalent bond.

3. True/False. Na_2SO_4 contains only ionic and covalent bonds.

4. True/False.   The dipole moment of NH_3 is higher than that of NF_3.

5. True/False.   In cyanide ion, the negative charge resides on nitrogen.

6. The percent ionic character using dipole moment is calculated by _________________.

7. AgI is ___________ covalent than KI.

8. $AlCl_3$ has contraction/expansion of octet.

9. The dipole moment of BCl_3 is _____________ while that of PCl_3 is _____________.

10. Formation of ionic bond is favoured by _________________________________.

ANSWERS TO PROFICIENCY TEST– I

1. True

2. False

3. False

4. True

5. False

6. $\left(\dfrac{\text{Observed dipole moment}}{\text{Calculated dipole moment}} \times 100\right)$

7. More

8. Contraction

9. Zero, non–zero

10. Low ionization potential of metal, high electron affinity of non–metal, low dissociation enthalpy, low sublimation energy and high lattice energy of the crystal.

6 MOLECULAR GEOMETRY AND VSEPR THEORY

Molecular geometry is the three–dimensional arrangement of atoms in a molecule.
A molecule's geometry affects its physical and chemical properties such as melting point, boiling point and the types of reactions it undergoes. In general, bond length and bond angles are determined by experiments. However, there is a simple procedure to predict the overall geometry of a molecule or ion with considerable accuracy, if we know the number of electrons surrounding a central atom in its Lewis structure. The basis of this approach is the assumption that electron pairs in the valence shell (outermost electron–occupied shell of an atom) of an atom repel one another. In a polyatomic species, the repulsion between electrons in different bonding pairs causes them to remain as far as possible. Thus, the geometry assumed by the species ultimately minimizes the repulsion. This approach is called valence–shell electron–pair repulsion (VSEPR) theory because it accounts for the geometric arrangements of electron pairs around a central atom in terms of the electrostatic repulsion between electron pairs.

Molecules in this theory are divided into two categories, depending on whether the central atom has lone pair of electrons or not.

7.1   Molecules in which the central atom has no lone pairs.

For simplicity, we will consider molecules that contain only two types of atoms, A and B, of which A is the central atom. These molecules have the general formula AB_x, where x is an integer 2, 3 .....(if x = 1, the molecule will be diatomic, which is linear by definition).

(a) Molecules having general formula AB_2

$BeCl_2$ is representing the general formula AB_2. The Lewis structure of beryllium chloride in the

gaseous state is

$$: \ddot{Cl} \rightleftharpoons Be \rightleftharpoons \ddot{Cl} :$$
$$180°$$

Since the bonding pairs repel each other, they must be at opposite ends of a straight line in order for them to be as far apart as possible. Thus, ClBeCl bond angle is predicted to be 180° and the molecule is *linear*.

(b) Molecules having general formula AB_3

The general formula AB_3 is represented by the molecule BF_3. BF_3 has three bonding pairs, which points to the corners of an equilateral triangle with boron at the center of the triangle.

$$\begin{array}{c} :\ddot{F}: \\ | \;120° \\ B \\ \diagup \quad \diagdown \\ :\ddot{F} \qquad \ddot{F}: \end{array}$$

This geometry of BF_3 is referred as ***trigonal planar*** with FBF bond angle to be 120°. In this structure, all four atoms lie in the same plane,

(c) Molecules having general formula AB_4

Methane (CH_4) represents the best example of this class of molecules. The Lewis structure of CH_4

is
$$\begin{array}{c} H \\ | \\ H - C - H \\ | \\ H \end{array}$$

The four bonding pairs in CH_4 can be arranged to form a tetrahedron, so as to minimize the repulsion between them. A tetrahedron has four faces, all of which are equilateral triangles.
In a ***tetrahedral*** molecule, the central atom (carbon) is located at the center of the tetrahedron and the other four atoms (H) are at the corners. The HCH bond angles are all 109°28'.

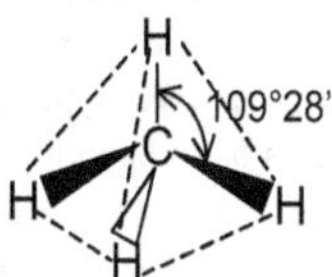

(d) Molecules with general formula AB_5

The general formula AB_5 is represented by the molecule PCl_5. The Lewis structure of PCl_5 (in gas phase) is

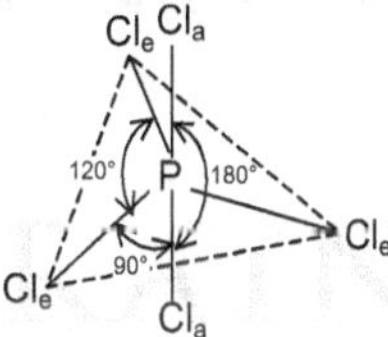

The only way to minimize the repulsive forces among the five bonding pairs is to arrange the P–Cl bonds in the form of a ***trigonal bipyramid***. Joining two tetrahedrons along a common triangular base can generate a trigonal bipyramid.

The central atom (P) is at the center of the common triangular with the surrounding atoms positioned at the five corners of the trigonal bipyramid. The atoms that are above and below the triangular plane are said to occupy axial positions and those, which are in the triangular plane, are said to occupy equatorial positions. The angle between any two equatorial bonds is 120°, that between an axial bond and an equatorial bond is 90° and that between two axial bonds is 180°.

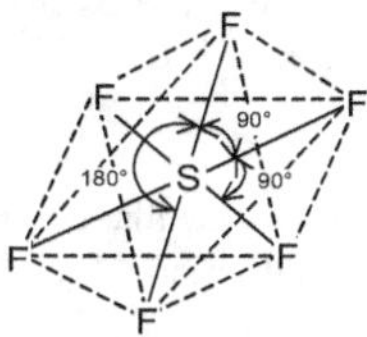

(e) Molecules having general formula AB_6

The molecule SF_6 exhibits the general formula AB_6. The Lewis structure of SF_6 is

The most stable arrangement of the six S–F bonding pairs is in the shape of an ***octahedron***. An octahedron has eight faces and can be generated by joining two square pyramids on a common base. The central atom (S) is at the center of the square base and the surrounding atoms (F) are at the six corners. All bond angles are 90° except the one made by the bonds between the central atom and the pairs of atoms that are diametrically opposite to each other, which is 180°. Since, all the bonds are equivalent in an octahedral molecule, the terms axial and equatorial are not used here.

7.2　　MOLECULES IN WHICH THE CENTRAL ATOM HAS ONE OR MORE LONE PAIRS

In such molecules, there are three types of repulsive interactions–between bonding pairs, between lone pairs and between a bonding pair and a lone pair. In general, according to VSEPR theory, the repulsive forces decrease in the following order: lone pair–lone pair repulsion > lone pair – bond pair repulsion > bond pair – bond pair repulsion.

Bond pair electrons are held by the attractive forces exerted by the nuclei of the two bonded atoms. These electrons have less "spatial distribution" than lone pairs i.e., they take up less space than lone pair electrons, which are associated with only one nuclei (or one atom). Because lone–pair electrons in a molecule occupy more space, they experience greater repulsion from neighbouring lone pairs and bonding pairs.

To keep track of total number of bonding pairs and lone pairs, we designate molecules with lone pairs as AB_xE_y, where A is the central atom, B is the surrounding atoms and E is a lone pair on A. Both x and y are integers, $x = 2, 3…..$ and $y = 1, 2 …..$ Thus, x and y denote the number of surrounding atoms and number of lone pairs on the central atom, respectively.

(a)　　**Molecules with general formula AB_2E**

Example of this type is SO_2. The Lewis structure of SO_2 is $:\overset{..}{O}\!=\!\overset{\oplus}{\underset{..}{S}}\!-\!\overset{\ominus}{\underset{..}{O}}:$

VSEPR theory treats double bond and triple bonds as though they were single bonds. Thus, SO_2 molecule can be viewed as having three electron pairs on the central atoms, of which, two are bonding pairs and one is a lone pair. The overall arrangement of three electron pairs is trigonal planar. But since one of the electron pair is a lone pair, the SO_2 molecule looks like

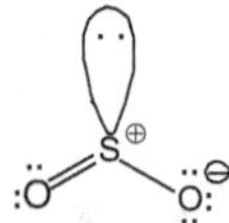

This shape is referred as ***bent or angular***. The shape is determined only by the bonding pairs and not by lone pairs. Since lone pair repels the bonding pairs more strongly, the SO bonds are pushed together slightly and the OSO angle is less than 120°.

(b) Molecules having general formula AB_3E

The general formula AB_3E is exhibited by the molecule NH_3. Ammonia has overall four electron pairs, of which three are bonding pairs and one is lone pair. The overall arrangement of four electron pairs is tetrahedral but since one of the electron pairs is a lone pair, so the shape of NH_3 is ***trigonal pyramidal.*** Because the lone pairs repels the bonding pairs more strongly, the three N–H bonds are pushed closer together. Thus the HNH bond angle is smaller than the ideal tetrahedral angle of 109°28'.

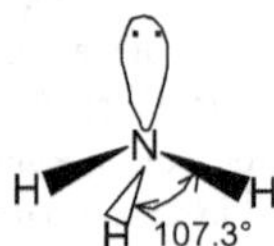

(c) Molecules with general formula AB_2E_2

Example of such a molecule is H_2O. A water molecule has 2 bonding pairs and two lone pairs

$$H—\overset{..}{\underset{..}{O}}—H　.$$

The overall arrangement of the four electron pairs in water is tetrahedral. However, unlike NH_3, H_2O has 2 lone pairs on the central O atom. These lone pairs tend to be as far from each other as possible. Consequently, the two OH bonding pairs are pushed toward each other and H_2O shows even greater deviation from tetrahedral angle than in NH_3. The shape of H_2O is referred as *bent or angular* with HOH bond angle of 104.5°.

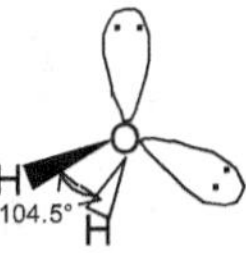
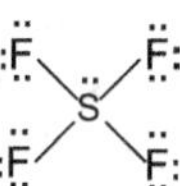

(d) Molecules having general formula AB₄E

Example to this class of molecule is SF_4. The Lewis structure of SF_4 is

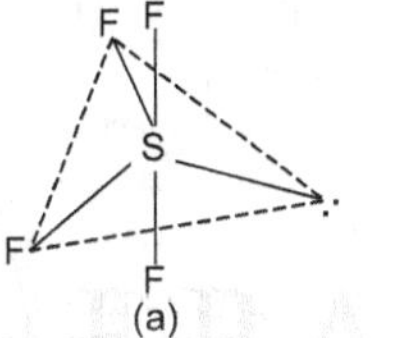

The S atom in SF_4 has 5 electron pairs, which can be arranged as trigonal bipyramidal.
In SF_4, since one of the electron pair is a lone pair, so the molecule can have any one of the following geometries:

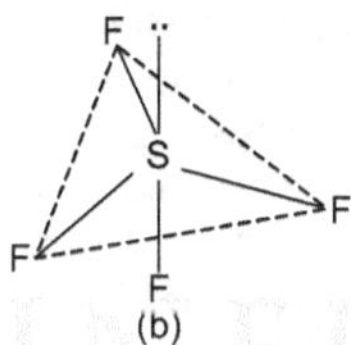

(a)   (b)

In (a), the lone pair occupies an equatorial position and in (b), it occupies an axial position. Repulsion between the electrons pairs in bonds only 90° apart are greater than repulsion between electron pairs in bonds 120° apart. Each axial bond has three electron pairs 90° away while each equatorial bond has only two electron pairs 90° away. Thus axial bonds (electron pairs) experience greater repulsion than the equatorial bonds. Thus, atoms at the equatorial positions are closer to the central atom than atoms at the axial positions i.e. equatorial bond lengths are smaller than axial bond lengths. Thus, when the central atom also has lone pairs along with the bonding pairs, it will occupy a position where the repulsions are less, so lone pairs in trigonal bipyramidal are more comfortable at equatorial positions. Thus, (a) is the appropriate structure of SF_4. It is referred as *see–saw shaped or irregular tetrahedron.*

(e) Molecules with general formula AB₃E₂

Example of this type is ClF_3. The Lewis structure of ClF_3 is

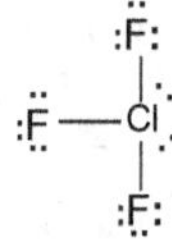

The Cl atom in ClF_3 has 5 electron pairs, of which 2 are lone pairs and 3 are bonding pairs. The molecule can have any of the following three geometries:

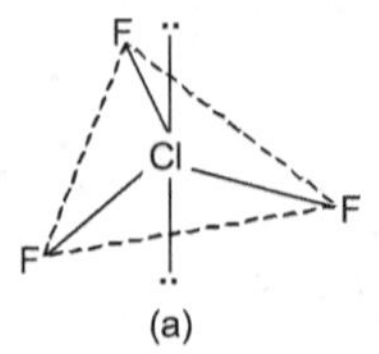

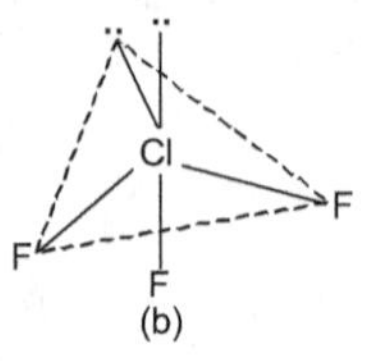

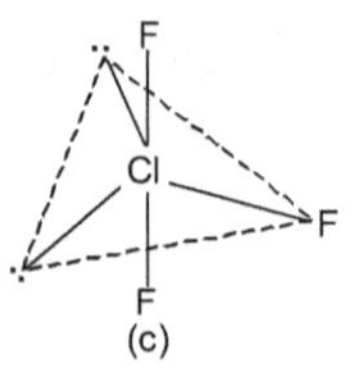

In structure (a), there are 6 lone pair–bond pair repulsions at 90° and one lone pair – lone pair repulsion at 180°. In structure (b), 1 lone pair – lone pair repulsion is at 90° and there are 3 lone pair–bond pair repulsions at 90°, 2 at 120° and 1 at 180°. While in structure

(c), there are 4 lone pair–bond pair repulsions at 90°, 2 at 120° and one lone pair–lone pair repulsion at 120°. The structure (b) is out rightly ruled out since the lone pair–lone pair repulsion is of highest magnitude. Among structures (a) and (c), each structure has 4 lone pair–bond pair repulsions at 90°. Apart from these repulsions, (a) has 1 lone pair–lone pair repulsion at 180° and 2 lone pair–bond pair repulsions at 90° while

(c) has 1 lone pair–lone pair repulsion at 120° & 2 lone pair–bond pair repulsions also at 120°. So, the structure (c) has overall lesser repulsions than (a). Thus, (c) is the appropriate structure of ClF_3. It is called ***T–shaped*** structure.

7.3   PREDICITING GEOMETRY OF SPECIES USING VSEPR THEORY

With the help of VSEPR theory, we can predict the geometry of various species in a systematic way. The scheme makes use of the following steps:

(i)   Identify the central atom and count the number of valence electrons on the central atom.

(ii)   Add to this, the number of other atoms (which form single bonds only). Here, oxygen atoms are not added as they form two bonds.

(iii)   If the species is an anion, add negative charges and if it is a cation, subtract positive charges.

(iv)   This gives us a number, which we refer as N.

(v)   Divide N by 2 and we get the sum of bonding and non–bonding electron pairs.

$$\frac{N}{2} = \text{Number of other atoms + number of lone pairs.}$$

(vi)   Compare the result $\left(\frac{N}{2} \text{ value}\right)$ with the value given in table, corresponding to the given

number of lone pairs.

N/2 value	No. of lone pairs	Shape of the species	Example
2	0	Linear	$HgCl_2$, $BeCl_2$
3	0	Triangular planar	BF_3, $AlCl_3$, BH_3, NO_3^-, SO_3
	1	Angular or bent	$SnCl_2$, SO_2, NO_2^-
4	0	Tetrahedral	CCl_4, BeF_4^{2-}, BF_4^-, PCl_4^+, ClO_4^-
	1	Trigonal pyramidal	NH_3, PCl_3, PF_3, ClO_3^-
	2	Angular or bent	H_2O, H_2S, OF_2, ClO_2^-
	3	Linear	ClO^-
5	0	Trigonal bipyramidal	PCl_5, PF_5
	1	See–saw or irregular tetrahedron	SF_4, IF_4^+
	2	T–shaped	ClF_3, BrF_3

	3		Linear	I_3^-, Br_3^-, XeF_2
6	0		Octahedral or square bipyramidal	SF_6, PCl_6^-
	1		Square pyramidal	BrF_5, IF_5
	2		Square planar	ICl_4^-, XeF_4, IF_4
7	0		Pentagonal bipyramidal	IF_7

Note: XeF_6 does not have octahedral structure. It's structure is *capped octahedron*.

Let us see the usefulness of the VSEPR theory to predict the geometry of few molecules/ ions.

(i) $BeCl_2$ molecule:

The central atom is Be and it has two other Cl atoms.

$$\therefore \ \frac{N}{2} = \frac{2+2}{2} = 2$$

Since, the number of other atoms are 2, so the number of lone pairs are zero. Thus, shape of $BeCl_2$ is *linear.*

$$Cl\!\!-\!\!-\!\!Be\!\!-\!\!-\!\!Cl$$

(ii) BF_3 molecule:

In BF_3, central atom is boron and it has three other atoms.

$$\therefore \ \frac{N}{2} = \frac{3+3}{2} = 3$$

Since, the number of other atoms are three, so the number of lone pairs are zero. Therefore, shape is *triangular planar.*

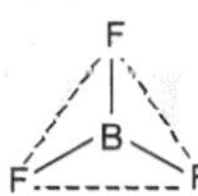

(iii) NO_2^- ion:

The central atom in NO_2^- is N and it has two other atoms.

$$\therefore \ \frac{N}{2} = \frac{5+1}{2} = 3$$

Since, the number of other atoms are 2, so the number of lone pairs would be 1. Thus, shape of NO_2^- ion is *angular or bent.*

(iv) BeF_4^{2-} ion:

In BeF_4^{2-}, the central atom is Be and it has four other F atoms.

$$\therefore \ \frac{N}{2} = \frac{2+4+2}{2} = 4$$

The number of lone pairs are zero, as the number of other atoms are 4. Therefore, shape of BeF_4^{2-} is *tetrahedral.*

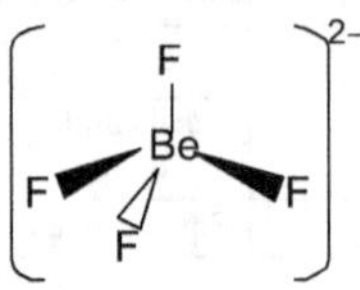

(v) NH_3 molecule:

In NH_3, the central atom is N and it has 3 other H atoms.

$$\therefore \ \frac{N}{2} = \frac{5+3}{2} = 4$$

Since, the number of other atoms is 3, so the number of lone pairs would be 1. Therefore, shape of NH_3 molecule is *trigonal pyramidal.*

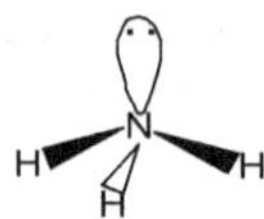

(vi) H_2S molecule:

The central atom is S and there are 2 other H atoms in H_2S molecule.

$$\therefore \ \frac{N}{2} = \frac{6+2}{2} = 4$$

Since, the number of other atoms is 2, so the number of lone pairs would be 2. Thus, the shape of H_2S is *angular or bent.*

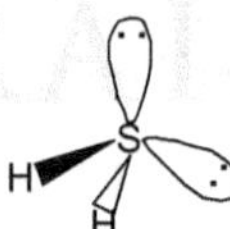

(vii) ClO^- ion:

The central atom is Cl and it has one other atom.

$$\therefore \ \frac{N}{2} = \frac{7+1}{2} = 4$$

The number of lone pairs would be 3 as the other atom is only one. Thus, the shape of ClO^- is *linear.*

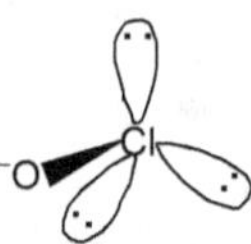

(viii) PCl_5 molecule:

The central atom in PCl_5 is P and it has 5 other Cl atoms.

$$\therefore \ \frac{N}{2} = \frac{5+5}{2} = 5$$

The number of lone pairs would be zero, as the number of other atoms is 5. Thus, the shape of PCl_5 is *trigonal bipyramidal.*

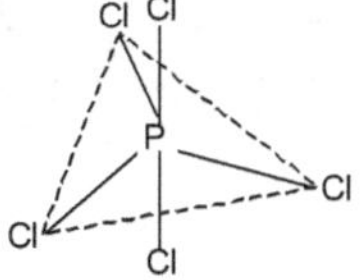

(ix) IF_4^+ ion:

The central atom in IF_4^+ ion is I and it has 4 other F atoms.

$$\therefore \frac{N}{2} = \frac{7+4-1}{2} = 5$$

Since, the number of other atoms is 4, so the number of lone pairs would be 1. Thus, the shape of IF_4^+ ion is *see–saw or irregular tetrahedron.*

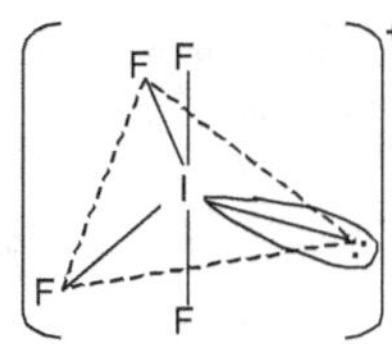

(x) BrF_3 molecule:

In BrF_3 molecule, the central atom is Br and it has 3 other F atoms.

$$\therefore \frac{N}{2} = \frac{7+3}{2} = 5$$

Since, the number of other atoms is 3, so the number of lone pairs is 2. Therefore, the shape of BrF_3 is *T–shaped.*

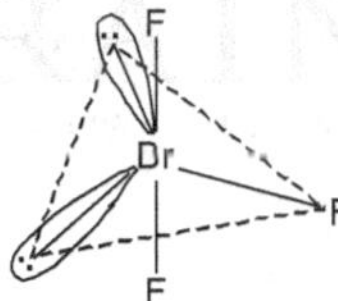

(xi) Br_3^- ion:

The central atom is a Br atom and it has 2 other Br atoms as surrounding atoms.

$$\therefore \frac{N}{2} = \frac{7+2+1}{2} = 5$$

Since, the number of other atoms is 2, so the number of lone pairs is 3. Thus, the shape of Br_3^- ion is *linear.*

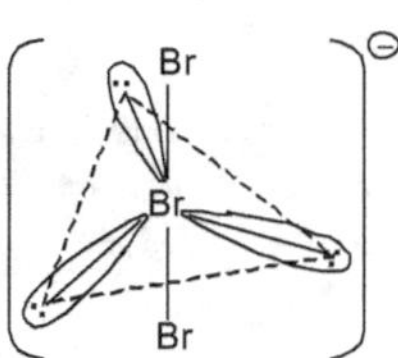

(xii) SF_6 molecule:

The central atom in SF_6 is S and it has 6 other F atoms as surrounding atoms.

$$\therefore \frac{N}{2} = \frac{6+6}{2} = 6$$

Since, the number of other atoms is 6, so the number of lone pairs are zero. Thus, the shape of SF_6 molecule is *octahedron or square bipyramidal.*

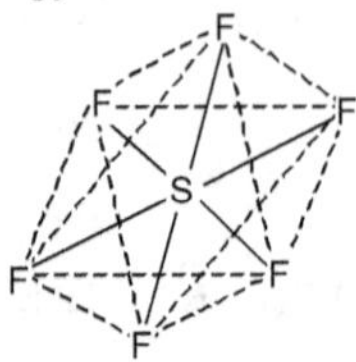

(xiii) BrF$_5$ molecule:

In BrF_5, the central atom is Br and 5 F atoms are the surrounding atoms.

$$\therefore \quad \frac{N}{2} = \frac{7+5}{2} = 6$$

Since, the number of other atoms is 5, so the number of lone pairs would be 1. Therefore, the shape of BrF_5 is *square pyramidal.*

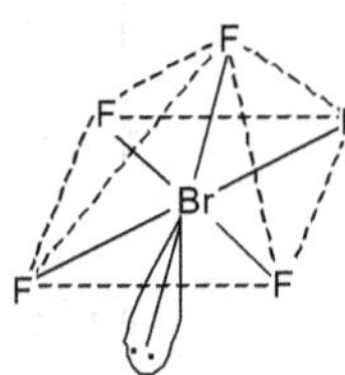

(xiv) ICl$_4^-$ ion:

In ICl_4^- ion, the central atom is I and 4 Cl atoms are the surrounding atoms.

$$\therefore \quad \frac{N}{2} = \frac{7+4+1}{2} = 6$$

The number of lone pairs would be 2 as the number of other atoms is 4. So, the shape of ICl_4^- ion is *square planar.*

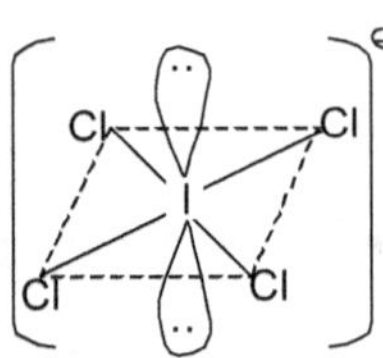

(xv) IF$_7$ molecule:

In IF_7 molecule, the central atom is I and 7 F atoms are the surrounding atoms.

$$\therefore \quad \frac{N}{2} = \frac{7+7}{2} = 7$$

Since, the number of other atoms is 7, so the number of lone pairs would be zero. Thus, the shape of IF_7 molecule is *pentagonal bipyramidal.*

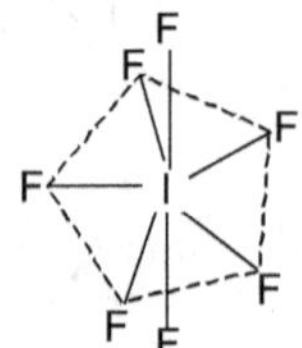

Illustration 6

Question: Write the geometry of XeF_4 and OSF_4 using VSEPR theory and clearly indicate the position of lone pair of electrons and hybridization of the central atom.

Solution:

XeF_4: $\dfrac{N}{2} = \dfrac{8+4}{2} = 6$

There are two lone pairs. Structure is octahedral and shape is square planar.

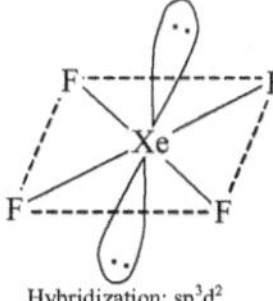

OSF_4: $\dfrac{N}{2} = \dfrac{6+4}{2} = 5$

Structure is irregular trigonal bipyramidal with less electronegative element occupying equitorial position. There is no lone pair.

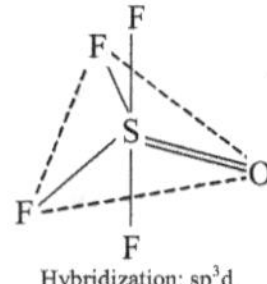

In addition to all this, VSEPR theory can also used to determine the geometry of other covalently bonded molecules and their bond angles. In order to predict these, following generalizations would be helpful.

1. Lone pair causes greater repulsions than a lone electron. For example,

$$O{=}N{=}O \quad 180° \qquad O{-}N{-}O \quad 134° \qquad O{-}N{-}O \quad 115°$$

2. Repulsions exerted by bond pair's decrease as the electronegativity of the bonded atom increases. For example,

$OH_2 (104.5°) > OF_2 (103.1°)$

$NH_3 (107.2°) > NF_3 (102.3°)$

$PI_3 (102°) > PBr_3 (101.0°) > PCl_3 (100.3°)$

$AsI_3 (101°) > AsBr_3 (100.5°) > AsCl_3 (98.4°)$

3. Repulsion between bonded electron pairs in filled shells is greater than those between electron pairs in incompleted shells.

$OH_2 (104.5°) \gg SH_2 (92°) > SeH_2 (91°) > TeH_2 (89.5°)$

$NH_3 (107.2°) \gg PH_3 (93.8°) > AsH_3 (91.8°) \gtrsim SbH_3 (91.3°)$

$N(CH_3)_3, 109° > P(CH_3)_3, 102.5° > As(CH_3)_3, 96°$

4. When an atom with a filled valence shell & one or more lone pairs is bonded to an atom with an incomplete valence shell, or a valence shell that can become complete by electron shifts, there is a tendency for the lone pairs to be partially transferred from the filled to the unfilled shell.

$PH_3 (93.3°) < PF_3 (97.7°)$

$AsH_3 (91.8°) < AsF_3 (102°)$

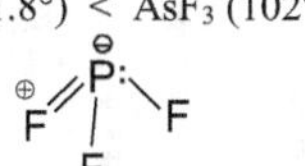

$Cl_2O (111°) > H_2O (104.5°) > F_2O (103.2°)$

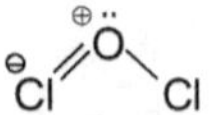

5. The size of a bonding electron pair decreases with increasing electronegativity of the ligand. Also, the two electron pairs of a double bond (or the three electron pairs of a triple bond) take up more room than does the one electron pair of a single bond.

   Using above facts one can rationalize size the trends which are given below:

Molecule	Angles		
	XCX	**XCO**	**XCC**
F_2CO	108°	126°	–
Cl_2CO	111°	124°	–
$(NH_2)_2CO$	118°	121°	–
F_2SO	93°	107°	–
$H_2C{=}CF_2$	110°	–	125°
OPF_3	103°	–	–
$OPCl_3$	104°	–	–
$H_2C{=}CCl_2$	114°	–	123°

7   SIGMA AND PIE BOND

Valence bond theory explains that a covalent bond is formed by the overlapping of the electron clouds of the atomic orbitals of the constituent atoms. The greater the overlap, the stronger the bond.

1. Formation of hydrogen molecule:

Hydrogen ($1s^1$) has only one electron in its 1s-orbital. When two hydrogen atoms come together, overlap of their s–orbitals takes place (s–s overlap), energy is released (bond energy) and a covalent bond called the σ bond is formed.

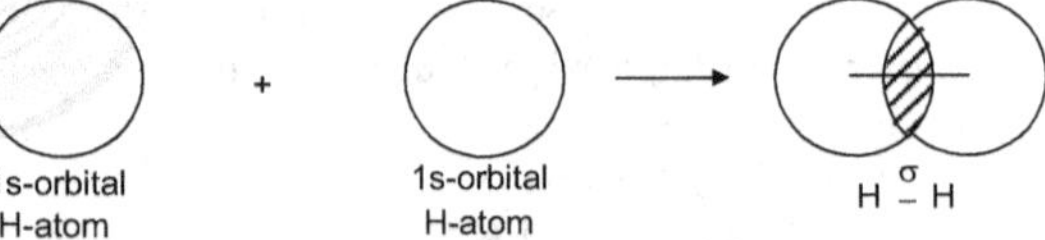

The electrons shared between the two atoms are to a large extent located in the region of space between the two nuclei. So the region of overlap is the region of high electron density. The electron density (or electron cloud) is distributed symmetrically about the bond axis, i.e., the line joining the nuclei. *Such a bond formed by the axial overlapping of the orbitals is called a sigma (σ) bond.*

2. Formation of hydrogen fluoride molecule:

      H $1s^1$ F $1s^2 2s^2 2p^5$

The 1s-orbital of the hydrogen atom and one of the 2p-orbitals of the fluorine atom contain only one electron each. The 1s–orbital of the hydrogen atom and the partly filled p–orbital of the fluorine atom overlap axially and form a σ bond (s–p overlap).

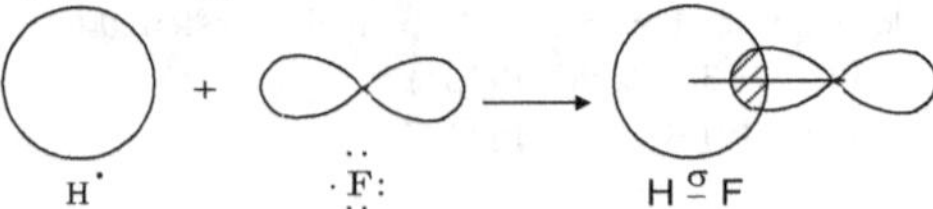

3.   **Formation of chlorine molecule:**

$$Cl \quad 1s^2 2s^2 2p^6 3s^2 3p^5$$

One of the 3p–orbitals of the chlorine atom contains only one electron. The half–filled p–orbital of a chlorine atom overlaps axially with the half-filled p–orbital of the other chlorine atom and forms a σ bond (p–p overlap).

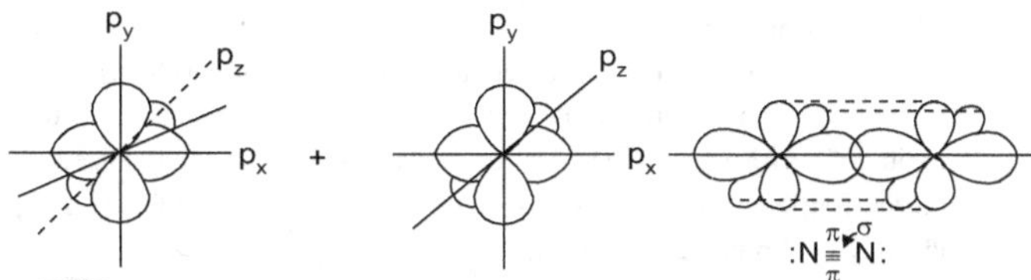

4.   **Formation of nitrogen molecule:**

$$N \qquad 1s^2 2s^2 \, 2p_x^1 \, 2p_y^1 \, 2p_z^1.$$

There are three unpaired electrons in the 2p–orbitals of a nitrogen atom. When two nitrogen atoms combine the three 2p–orbitals of one atom mutually overlap with those of the other atom and form three bonds.

Suppose the orbitals approach along the *x*-axis the p_x–orbitals overlap axially and form a σ bond (p – p overlap). The p_y and p_z–orbitals of the N atoms cannot overlap axially and so make a lateral (side to side) overlap forming two Pi (π) bonds.

Generally in any multiple bond between two atoms one bond is a σ bond and the others π bonds. A double bond will consist of a σ bond and a π bond and a triple bond will consist of a σ bond and two π bonds. In a π bond formed between two p-orbitals, the upper lobe overlaps the upper lobe and the lower lobe overlaps the lower lobe. Together they constitute π bond.

The π electron cloud will lie above and below the plane of the bond.

9   HYBRIDISATION

9.1   SP³ HYBRIDISATION

Carbon atom has the electronic configuration $1s^2 2s^2 \, 2p_x^1 \, 2p_y^1$. It has two half-filled orbitals.

It should be expected to show a covalency of 2. In its millions of compounds carbon shows tetracovalency. To explain this the concept of hybridisation is introduced. Consider the formation of methane, CH_4.

It may be supposed just for the sake of a picture that one of the electrons in the 2s-orbital is promoted to the vacant p_x orbital (excited state). This is possible because energy released during bond formation will compensate for this. Then the four orbitals, one s and three p-orbitals, get mixed up and form four new 'hybrid' orbitals, of equal energy which are called sp^3 hybrid orbitals, as they are formed by the mixing up (or blending) of one s and three p-orbitals.

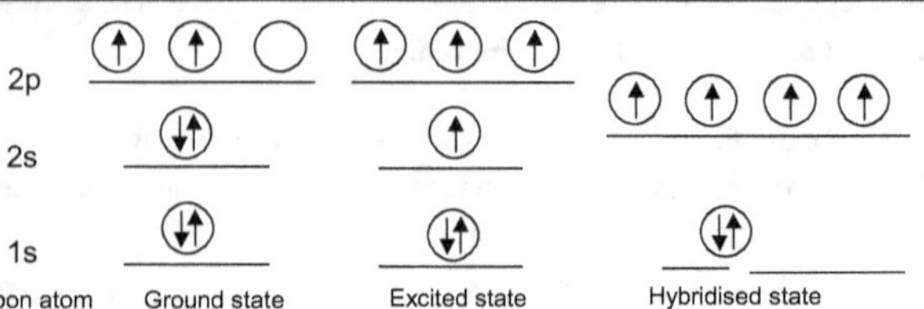

sp³ hybridisation of carbon atom

So hybridisation is nothing but *combination of a certain number of atomic orbitals of slightly different energies to form the same number of new (hybrid) orbitals of equal energy.*

sp³ hybrid orbital

Each sp³ hybrid orbital is like a p-orbital, but with 2 lobes of unequal size (In figures, the small lobe is usually omitted).

Since the hybrid orbitals repel one another, they orient themselves with an angle of 109°28′ between them and point to the four corners of a regular tetrahedron. Each hybridised orbital overlaps the 1s-orbital of a hydrogen atom and forms a σ bond. Each sp³ hybridised orbital has one fourth s character and three-fourths p character. Note that a hybrid atomic orbital from s and p-orbitals can form only σ bonds. (4 C – H σ bonds.)

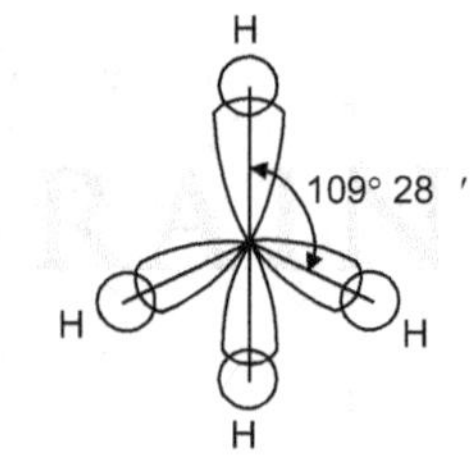

CH₄ molecule

Formation of Ethane: In this case there is sp³–sp³ overlap resulting in the formation of the C – C bond and sp³ – s overlap forming C – H bonds. (1 C – C σ bond and 6 C – H σ bonds.)

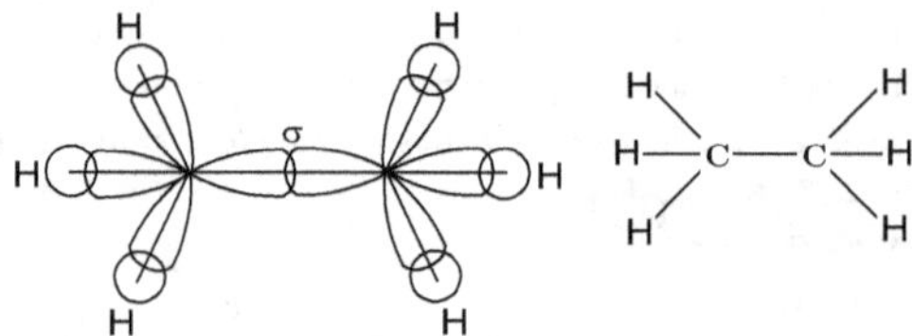

Formation of Ethane

9.2   SP² HYBRIDISATION

Formation of boron trifluoride/trichloride, BF₃/BCl₃

Boron has the electronic configuration $1s^2 2s^2 2p_x^1$. One of the s electrons is promoted to a vacant p_y–orbital (excited state). Then *one s-orbital and two p-orbitals* hybridise to form three sp² hybrid orbitals of equivalent energy. This kind of hybridisation is called *sp² (trigonal) hybridisation.*

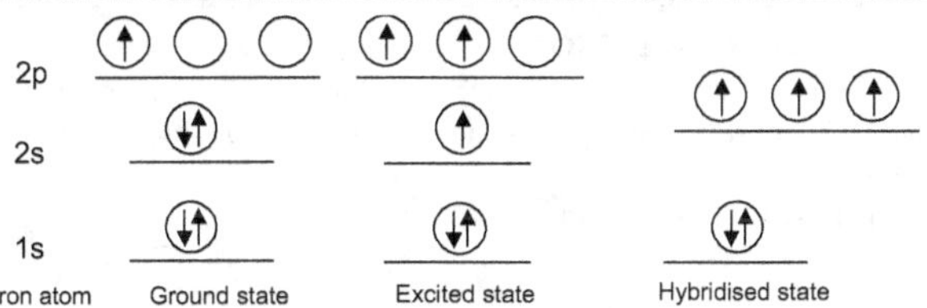

sp² hybridisation of Boron

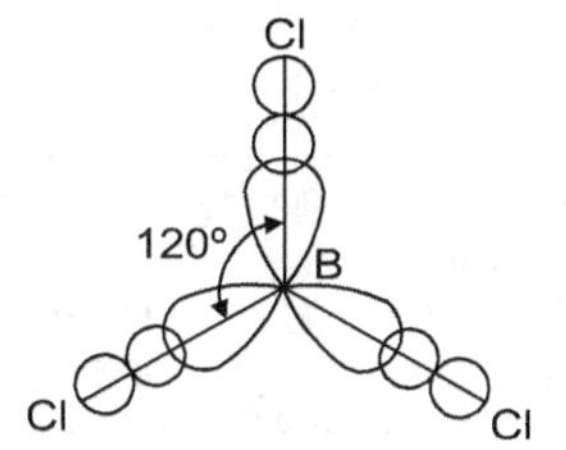

Formation of BCl₃

The three sp² hybrid orbitals are *co-planar* and are at angles of 120° to each other.
Each hybrid orbital overlaps with the vacant p-orbital of the chlorine atom and forms a σ bond. The other halides or Boron have similar structures. An sp² hybrid orbital has one-third s character and two-thirds p character. (3 σ bonds.)

Formation of Ethylene molecule

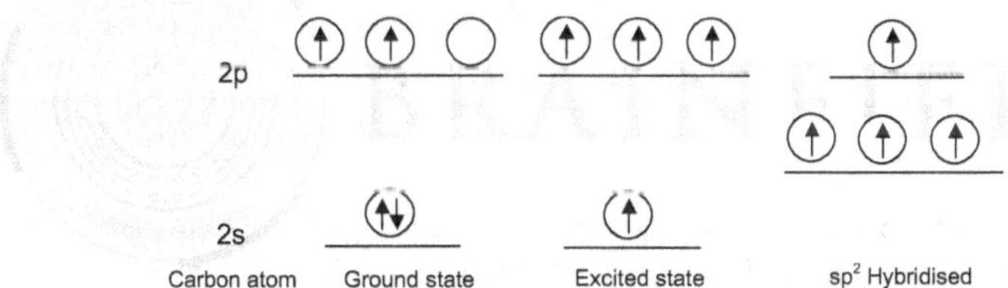

sp² hybridisation of carbon

In the formation of ethylene, carbon atom undergoes sp² hybridisation. Two of the sp² orbitals of each atom form σ bonds with 1s-orbitals of hydrogen atoms by axial overlapping.

The sp²–sp² overlap results in the formation of a C – C σ bond. The two carbon atoms and the four hydrogen atoms are all in the same plane and the bond angles are 120°.

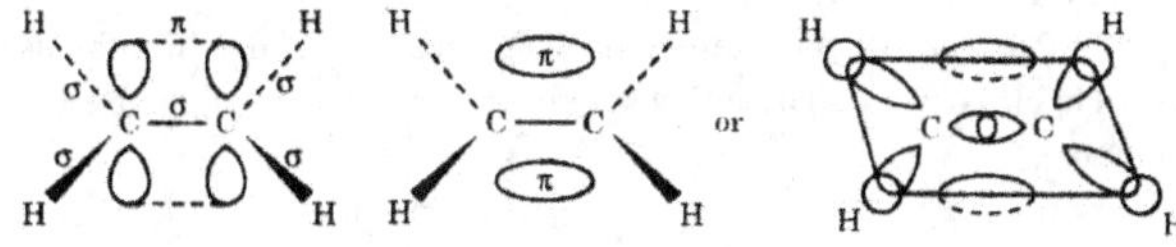

Ethylene molecule

At right angles to this plane there remains the $2p_z$, orbital of each carbon atom which overlap laterally to form a π bond between the two carbon atoms. The double bond between the two carbon atoms consists of a σ bond and a π bond. (4 C – H σ bonds, 1 C – C σ bond and 1 π bond)

9.3   SP HYBRIDISATION

One s and one p-orbital combine to form two hybrid orbitals known as sp (or linear or diagonal) orbitals. They are of equal energy and are collinear. Each sp-orbital has one-half s character and one-half p character.

(i)   Formation of beryllium chloride

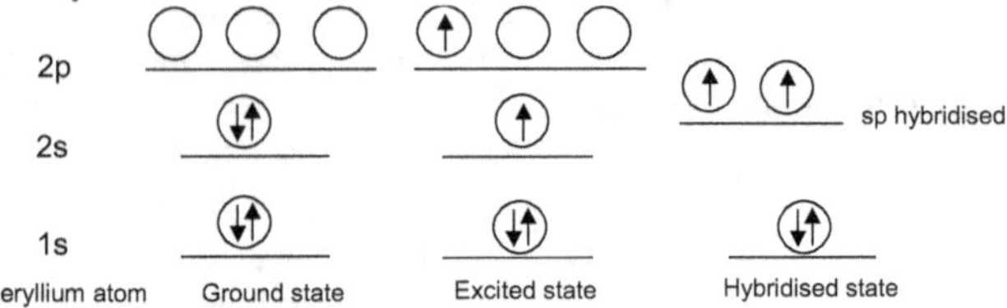

sp hybridization of Beryllium

The sp hybrid orbitals of beryllium atom overlap with the vacant p_x -orbitals of two chlorine atoms and form two σ bonds. Cl σ Be σ Cl since sp hybrid orbitals protrude along the axis farther than the corresponding s or p-orbitals they are able to overlap better and form stronger bonds than s or p-orbitals alone.

(ii)   Formation of acetylene

Hybridization of the one 2s and 2p carbon orbitals leads to the formation of two sp hybrid orbitals. sp–sp overlap between two carbon atoms form a σ bond between them. The other sp orbital on each carbon atom forms a σ bond with the 1s orbital of a hydrogen atom.

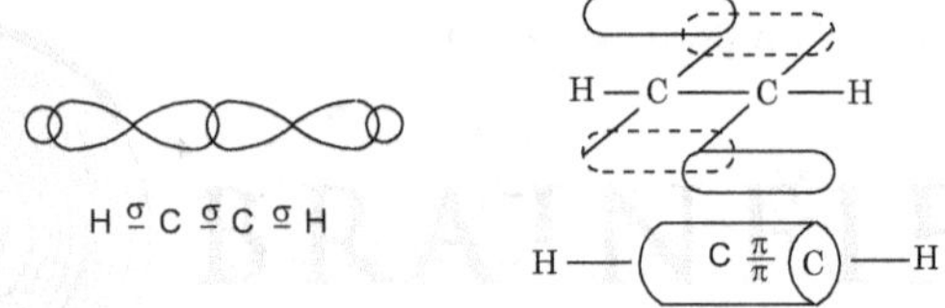

Acetylene molecule

Each of the carbon atom has two remaining p-orbitals which are mutually at right angles to each other. They laterally overlap and form two π bonds, sometimes pictured as a cylindrical sheath about the line joining the nuclei. One triple bond between 2 carbon atoms contains one C–C σ bond and 2π bonds. (1 C – C σ bond, 2 C – H σ bonds and 2π bonds)

The carbon-carbon triple bond is made up of one strong σ bond and two weaker π bonds; it has a total strength of 198 kcal/mole. It is stronger than a carbon-carbon double bond (163 kcal) or C–C single bond in ethane (88 kcal) and therefore is shorter than either.

9.4   sp³d HYBRIDIZATION

In this type of hybridization, one 's', three 'p' and one 'd' orbitals of the same shell mix to give five sp³d hybrid orbitals. These five sp³d hybrid orbitals orient themselves towards the corners of a trigonal bipyramidal.

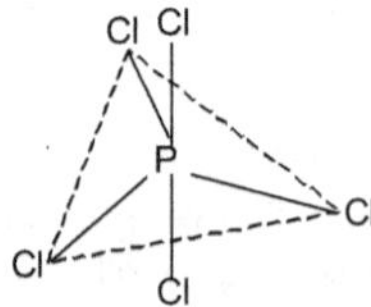

9.5   sp³d² HYBRIDIZATION

In this type of hybridization, one 's', three 'p' and two 'd' orbitals of the same/different shell mix to give six sp³d² hybrid orbitals. These six sp³d² hybrid orbitals orient themselves towards the corners of an octahedron. This type of hybridization is exhibited by SF_6, SCl_6 etc.

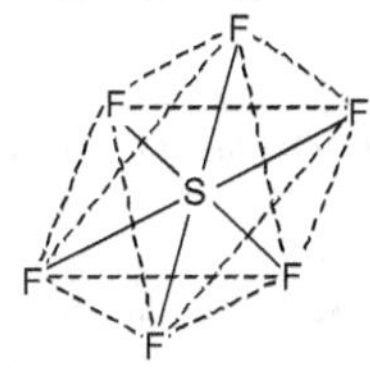

9.6 SCHEME FOR DETERMINING HYBRIDIZATION OF THE CENTRAL ATOM OF A SPECIES

(i) Identify the central atom of the species.

(ii) Write outermost electronic configuration of the central atom.

(iii) Determine oxidation state of the central atom.

(iv) Excite the electrons (if necessary) to the orbitals of higher energy in order to make the number of unpaired electrons equal to the oxidation state of the central atom.

(v) Now start putting orbitals into your pocket, beginning from 's' orbitals. The number of orbitals added to the pocket must have orbitals with unpaired electrons equal to number of other atoms of the species.

(vi) All the orbitals added to the pocket (including s orbital, whether it has paired or unpaired electrons) are now summed. If there are one 's' and one 'p' orbital in the pocket, then the hybridization is sp. If there are one 's' and '2p' orbitals in the pocket, it is sp^2 hybridization, and so on.

(vii) Each unpaired electron left (outside the pocket) will form a pi–bond.

(viii) Each orbital with paired electrons in the pocket will exist as lone pair on the central atom.

The working of this scheme can be seen in the following illustrations.

Illustration 7

Question: **Find out hybridization of the central atom in ClO_3^- and draw its structure.**

Solution:

(i) The central atom is Cl.

(ii) Outer most electron configuration of Cl = $[Ne]3s^2 3p^5$

(iii) Oxidation state of Cl is +5.

(iv) Outer most electron configuration of Cl after excitation:

(v) Now start adding orbitals into your pocket beginning from s, and thereafter 3p orbitals. We will stop adding orbitals to the pocket after adding all three '3p' orbitals because then the orbitals with unpaired electrons in the pocket would become equal to the number of other atoms in ClO_3^-.

(vi) So, the hybridization of Cl in ClO_3^- is sp^3.

(vii) Shape of ClO_3^- would be tetrahedral with one lone pair (pyramidal). Each unpaired electron left (outside the pocket) will form a π–bond and there will be one lone pair on Cl.

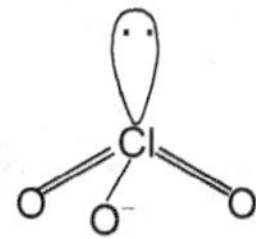

Illustration 8

Question: Find out hybridization of the central atom in ClO_2^- and draw its structure.

Solution:

(i) The central atom is Cl.

(ii) Outer most electron configuration of Cl = $[Ne]3s^2 3p^5$

$$\underset{3s}{\boxed{\uparrow\downarrow}} \quad \underset{3p}{\boxed{\uparrow\downarrow}\boxed{\uparrow\downarrow}\boxed{\uparrow}} \quad \underset{3d}{\boxed{}\boxed{}\boxed{}\boxed{}\boxed{}}$$

(iii) Oxidation state of Cl is +3.

(iv) Outer most electron configuration of Cl after excitation:

$$\underset{3s}{\boxed{\uparrow\downarrow}} \quad \underset{3p}{\boxed{\uparrow\downarrow}\boxed{\uparrow}\boxed{\uparrow}} \quad \underset{3d}{\boxed{\uparrow}\boxed{}\boxed{}\boxed{}\boxed{}}$$

(v) Now start adding orbitals into your pocket beginning from s, and thereafter 3p orbitals. We will stop adding orbitals to the pocket after adding all three '3p' orbitals because then the orbitals with unpaired electrons in the pocket would become equal to the number of other atoms in ClO_2^-.

(vi) So, the hybridization of Cl in ClO_2^- is sp^3.

(vii) Shape of ClO_2^- would be tetrahedral with two lone pairs (angular). Each unpaired electron left (outside the pocket) will form a π–bond and there will be two lone pair on Cl.

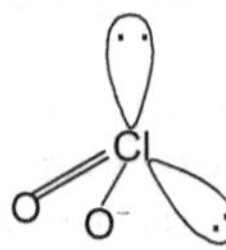

Illustration 9

Question: Find out hybridization of the central atom in ClO^- and draw its structure.

Solution:

(i) The central atom is Cl.

(ii) Outer most electron configuration of Cl = $[Ne]3s^2 3p^5$

$$\underset{3s}{\boxed{\uparrow\downarrow}} \quad \underset{3p}{\boxed{\uparrow\downarrow}\boxed{\uparrow\downarrow}\boxed{\uparrow}} \quad \underset{3d}{\boxed{}\boxed{}\boxed{}\boxed{}\boxed{}}$$

(iii) Oxidation state of Cl is +1.

(iv) There is no need for excitation of electrons because the number of unpaired electrons is already equal to oxidation state of Cl.

(v) Now start adding orbitals into your pocket beginning from s, and thereafter 3p orbitals. We will stop adding orbitals to the pocket after adding all three '3p' orbitals because then the orbitals with unpaired electrons in the pocket would become equal to the number of other atoms in ClO^-.

(vi) So, the hybridization of Cl in ClO^- is sp^3.

(vii) Shape of ClO^- would be tetrahedral with three lone pairs (linear). Chlorine atom will have three lone pairs.

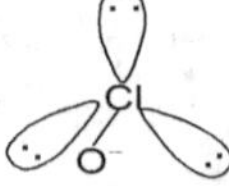

Illustration 10

Question: Find out hybridization of the central atom in SO_2 and draw its structure.

Solution:

(i) The central atom is S.

(ii) Outer most electron configuration of S = $[Ne]3s^2 3p^4$

3s   3p   3d

(iii) Oxidation state of S is +4.

(iv) Outer most electron configuration of S after excitation:

3s   3p   3d

(v) Now start adding orbitals into your pocket beginning from s, and thereafter 3p orbitals. We will stop adding orbitals to the pocket after adding two '3p' orbitals because then the orbitals with unpaired electrons in the pocket would become equal to the number of other atoms in SO_2.

(vi) So, the hybridization of S in SO_2 is sp^2.

(vii)Shape of SO_2 would be trigonal planar with one lone pair (angular). Each unpaired electron left (outside the pocket) will form a π–bond and there will be one lone pair on S.

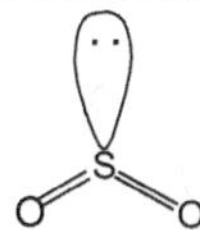

Illustration 11

Question: **Find out hybridization of the central atom in $XeOF_2$ and draw its structure.**

Solution:

(i) The central atom is Xe.

(ii) Outer most electron configuration of Xe is $5s^2 5p^6$

5s   5p   5d

(iii) Oxidation state of Xe is +4.

(iv) Outer most electron configuration of Xe after excitation:

5s   5p   5d

(v) Now start adding orbitals into your pocket beginning from s, and thereafter 5p orbitals and then d orbitals. We will stop adding orbitals to the pocket after all three '5p' orbitals and one '5d' orbital because then the orbitals with unpaired electrons in the pocket would become equal to the number of other atoms in $XeOF_2$.

(vi) So, the hybridization of Xe in $XeOF_2$ is sp^3d.

(vii)Shape of $XeOF_2$ would be trigonal bipyramidal with two lone pairs (T shaped). Each unpaired electron left (outside the pocket) will form a π–bond and there will be two lone pairs on Xe.

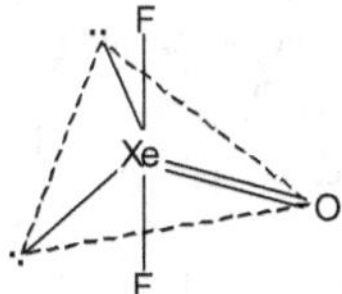

Illustration 12

Question: **Find out hybridization of the central atom in $XeOF_4$ and draw its structure.**

Solution:

(i) The central atom is Xe.

(ii) Outer most electron configuration of Xe is $5s^2 5p^6$

5s   5p   5d

(iii) Oxidation state of Xe is +6.

(iv) Outer most electron configuration of Xe after excitation:

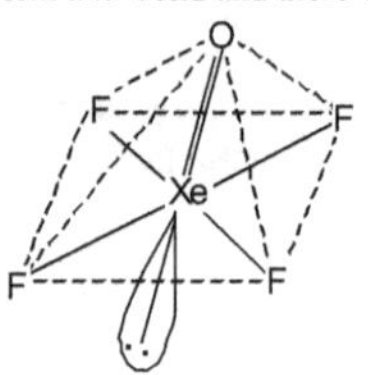

(v) Now start adding orbitals into your pocket beginning from s, and thereafter 5p orbitals and then d orbitals. We will stop adding orbitals to the pocket after all three '5p' orbitals and two '5d' orbital because then the orbitals with unpaired electrons in the pocket would become equal to the number of other atoms in $XeOF_4$.

(vi) So, the hybridization of Xe in $XeOF_4$ is sp^3d^2.

(vii) Shape of $XeOF_4$ would be octahedron with one lone pair (square pyramidal). Each unpaired electron left (outside the pocket) will form a π–bond and there will be one lone pair on Xe.

10 | HYDROGEN BOND

A hydrogen atom normally forms a single bond. In some compounds, however, the hydrogen atom may be located between two atoms acting as a bridge between them. Hydrogen atom is now involved in two bonds, one a normal covalent bond, the other a hydrogen bond.

A hydrogen bond is always formed between two small, strongly electronegative atoms such as fluorine, oxygen and nitrogen.

10.1 INTERMOLECULAR HYDROGEN BONDING – MOLECULAR ASSOCIATION

(i) Hydrogen fluoride:

From molecular measurements, it is known that hydrogen fluoride is associated (i.e., many molecules are joined together). HF is a polar molecule, with the fluorine atom acquiring a slight negative charge and the hydrogen atom acquiring an equal positive charge. The electrostatic attraction between the oppositely charged ends results in hydrogen bonding as shown below.

$$H - F \ldots H - F \ldots H - F \ldots$$

Many $H - F$ units are held together, as $(HF)_n$, by hydrogen bonding. The covalent $H - F$ bond is much shorter than the $F \ldots H$ hydrogen bond; so a hydrogen bond is much weaker than a covalent bond. Fluorine, with the highest electronegativity forms the strongest hydrogen bond. The nature of the hydrogen bond is considerably electrostatic.

(ii) Water: The high boiling point compared to that of hydrogen sulphide is due to molecular association through hydrogen bonding.

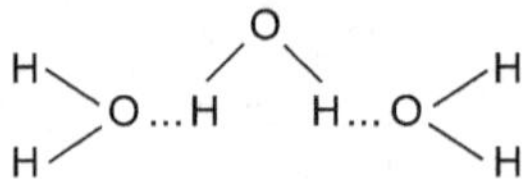

The crystal structure of ice shows a tetrahedral arrangement of water molecules.

Each oxygen atom is surrounded tetrahedrally by 4 others. Hydrogen bonds link pairs of oxygen atoms together as shown in Figure 6.19. The arrangement of water molecules in ice is a very open structure and this explains the low density of ice. When ice melts, the structure breaks down and the molecules pack more closely together so that water has a higher density; this packing goes to a maximum upto a temperature of 4°C.

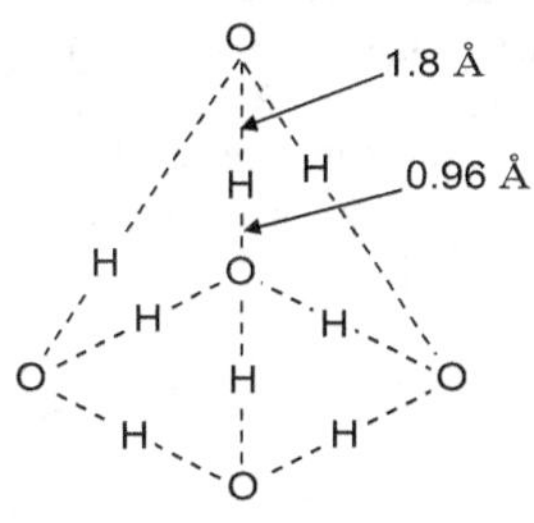

(iii) Ammonia is also associated through hydrogen bonding; hence it has higher boiling point than PH_3 or AsH_3.

Note: Methane has normal values for its melting and boiling points. It is not associated as carbon has no lone pairs and is not sufficiently electronegative to be linked by hydrogen bonds.

(iv) Alcohols and phenols: Lower alcohols and phenols are associated due to intermolecular hydrogen bonding. Methanol, ethanol and phenol have relatively much higher boiling points than methane or chloromethane, ethane or chloroethane, benzene or chlorobenzene respectively.

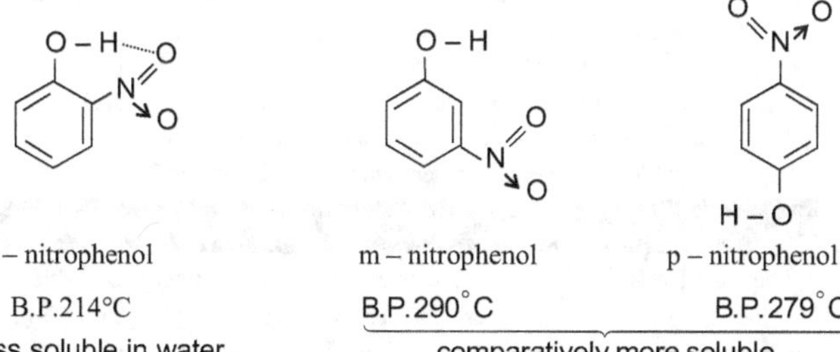

(v) Carboxylic acids: Some carboxylic acids exist as dimers e.g., the dimer of acetic acid is represented as

In aqueous solution molecules of a carboxylic acid link up with water molecules through hydrogen bonding rather than form dimers.

10.2 INTRAMOLECULAR HYDROGEN BONDING

Sometimes hydrogen bonding may take place within a molecule; this is known as intramolecular (or internal) hydrogen bonding. It may lead to the linkage of two groups to form a ring; such an effect is known as chelation, in the case of complex compounds.

(i) Nitrophenols

o – nitrophenol   m – nitrophenol   p – nitrophenol

B.P. 214°C   B.P. 290°C   B.P. 279°C

less soluble in water   comparatively more soluble

Because of the proximity of – OH and – NO_2 groups in o-nitrophenol there is intramolecular hydrogen bonding which prevents intermolecular hydrogen bonding between two or more molecules. Since molecular association cannot take place, the boiling point of o-nitrophenol is lower than that of the other two. Because of the distance between –OH and –NO_2 groups in m– and p–nitrophenols there is no possibility of intramolecular hydrogen bonding. Intermolecular hydrogen bonding may take place to a certain extent which causes some degree of molecular association; this is responsible for the higher boiling points of the two nitrophenols.

Further the formation of intramolecular hydrogen bonding in o-nitrophenol prevents it from entering into intermolecular hydrogen bonding with water and this explains its reduced solubility.

(ii) Other molecules in which intramolecular hydrogen bonding is present are o-hydroxybenzaldehyde, o-chlorophenol and o-hydroxybenzoic acid.

Illustration 13

Question: **H_2O is a liquid at ordinary temperature while H_2S is a gas although both O and S belong to the same group of the periodic table.**

Solution: H_2O is capable of forming intermolecular hydrogen bond. This is possible due to high electronegativity and small size of oxygen. Due to intermolecular H–bonding, molecular association takes place. As a result the effective molecular weight increases and hence the boiling point increases, so H_2O exist in liquid phase. But in H_2S, no hydrogen bonding is possible due to large size and less electronegativity of S. So it's boiling point is that of an isolated H_2S molecule and therefore it is a gas with low boiling point.

Illustration 14

Question: **The salt KHF_2 is known but $KHCl_2$ is not known. Explain.**

Solution: The formation of KHF_2 involves reaction of HF_2^- with KOH. Similar is the case with $KHCl_2$. So the main factor is the formation of HF_2^- or HCl_2^- ion.

$$H - F + F^- \longrightarrow F\!\!-\!\!H\cdots F^-$$

$$H - Cl + Cl^- \longrightarrow Cl\!\!-\!\!H\cdots Cl^- \text{ (not possible)}$$

Due to higher electronegativity and small size of fluorine, it is capable of forming H–bond resulting in the formation of HF_2^- and thereby KHF_2 exists. But with chlorine, there is no possibility of H–bonding, so there is no possibility of existence of $KHCl_2$.

Illustration 15

Question: **o–hydroxy benzaldehdye is more volatile than p–hydroxy benzaldehyde.**

Solution: More volatiliity means compound has lower boiling point. p–hydroxy benzaldehyde remains associated through intermolecular hydrogen bonding. But in o–hydroxy benzaldehyde, intramolecular H–bonding takes places, as a result of which there is no association.

So p–hydroxy benzaldehyde, which remains as an associated species has got higher boiling and so less volatile while o–hydroxy benzaldehyde is highly volatile.

11 MOLECULAR ORBITAL THEORY AND BOND ORDER

The Valance Bond Theory (V.B. Theory) with the concepts of hybridisation and resonance is used to explain the structure and properties of several molecules, but there are limitations. For example, the V.B. theory in its original form, is not able to explain the paramagnetic behaviour of O_2 molecule. Hence the Molecular Orbital Theory (or M.O. Theory) due to Hund and Mulliken. The following are the essential features of the M.O. Theory.

1. In the M.O. model, all the electrons are taken together and considered as moving in the field of all the nuclei. (In the V.B. model, only the bonding electrons are considered and they are taken to move in the field of the nuclei involved in bonding.)

2. The atomic orbitals are combined to form, what are called molecular orbitals and electrons are fed into these orbitals. (In the V.B. model, electrons are fed into the atomic orbitals, which are then supposed to overlap.)

3. The number of combining atomic orbitals is equal to the number of molecular orbitals formed.

4. When two atomic orbitals combine, two M.O's are formed, of which one has a lower energy, while the other has a higher energy. The former is known as the bonding orbital and the latter antibonding. Mathematically, if ψ_1 represents the wave function corresponding to orbital 1 and ψ_2 for orbital 2, the total function is a linear combination of ψ_1 and ψ_2 i.e., $\psi = \psi_1 \pm \psi_2$ (omitting the constants). This is known as linear combination of atomic orbitals (L.C.A.O.). Of these, $\psi_1 + \psi_2$ corresponds to the bonding M.O., while $\psi_1 - \psi_2$ corresponds to antibonding M.O. i.e., $\psi_b = \psi_1 + \psi_2$ and $\psi_a = \psi_1 - \psi_2$. The electron density or probability of finding an electron is directly proportional to ψ^2.

For the bonding orbital, $\psi_b^2 = (\psi_1 + \psi_2)^2 = \psi_1^2 + \psi_2^2 + 2\psi_1\psi_2$, which is greater than $\psi_1^2 + \psi_2^2$ i.e., the electron density between the two nuclei is concentrated when the bonding M.O. is formed, than when no such combination of orbitals is made.

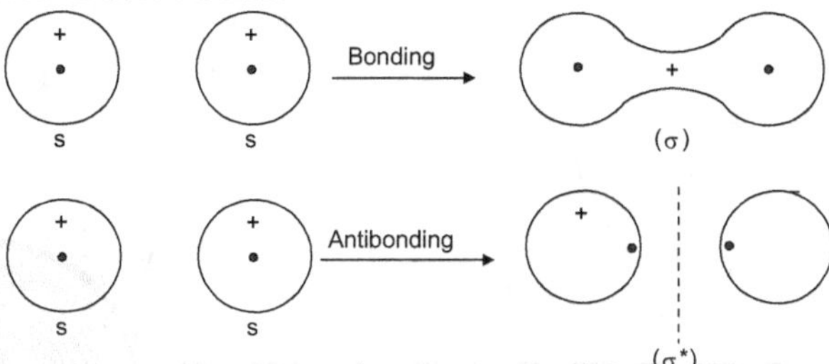

For the antibonding orbital, $\psi_a^2 = (\psi_1 - \psi_2)^2 = \psi_1^2 + \psi_2^2 - 2\psi_1\psi_2$, which is less than $\psi_1^2 + \psi_2^2$ i.e. the electron density between the nuclei is withdrawn in an antibonding M.O. In the bonding M.O., since the electron density between the two nuclei is large, it holds the two nuclei together; hence the name bonding orbital; in the antibonding M.O. the bonding of the nuclei is poor.

5. There are different notations for representing bonding and anti-boding M.O's obtained from A.O's. We give a simple notation below.

Atomic orbitals that are mixed	s and s	p_z and p_z	p_x and p_x	p_y and p_y
Bonding M.O.	σs	$\sigma(p_z)$	$\pi(p_x)$	$\pi(p_y)$
Antibonding M.O.	σ*s	$\sigma^*(p_z)$	$\pi^*(p_x)$	$\pi^*(p_y)$

We have assumed the two p_z orbitals to overlap end to end, so that the M.O. formed is of the 'σ' type (similar to the 'σ' bond in V.B. theory); then the two p_x atomic orbitals, as also the two p_y orbitals will overlap laterally to give M.O's of the π type. Some authors follow the convention of choosing two p_x orbitals for end to end (i.e., axial) overlap, so that the M.O's formed are $\sigma(p_x)$ and $\sigma^*(p_x)$.

6. When electrons are successively placed in the M.O's, Aufbau principle, Hund's rule and Pauli's principle are followed, as in the case of the atomic orbitals.
Aufbau Principle: M.O's are occupied in the order of increasing energy. The following is the general arrangement of M.O's in the order of increasing energy.
$\sigma(1s) < \sigma^*(1s) < \sigma(2s) < \sigma^*(2s) < \sigma(2p_z) < \pi(2p_x) = \pi(2p_y) < \pi^*(2p_x) = \pi^*(2p_y) < \sigma^*(2p_z)$ ... etc.

The above is only a general order and slight variations often occur due to interaction between s and p orbitals. For example, sometimes, $\pi(2p_x) = \pi(2p_y) < \sigma(2p_z)$.

7. **Hund's rule of maximum multiplicity:**
   The degenerate M.O's are occupied singly, before any pairing could occur. The maximum capacity for each M.O. is 2 electrons.

8. Only atomic orbitals of equal or nearly equal energies combine to give the M.O's. In the case of homonuclear diatomic molecules, energies of corresponding A.O's of the two atoms are equal. So the above condition of combination of A.O's assumes special significance in the case of heteronuclear diatomic molecules and it has to be used with caution.

   Further, for effective combination or overlap, the A.O's should have the same symmetry. Thus we have the s– s, p_z– p_z, p_y–p_y and p_x –p_x overlaps to give bonding and antibonding orbitals as pointed out earlier (see point 5). Regarding the s – p overlap, a 2s orbital may overlap with a $2p_z$ orbital as shown in Figure (a) below, since both have axial symmetry around the internuclear axis. However, the $2s$–$2p_x$ or $2s$–$2p_y$ overlap makes no contribution to bonding, as shown in Figure (b) below, where the constructive overlap in one region is exactly cancelled by the effect of the destructive overlap in the other.

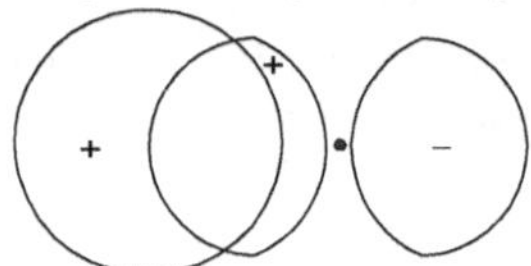

(a)   Enhanced amplitude

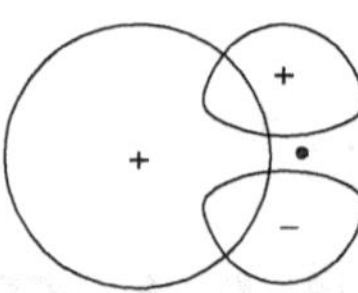

(b)   Decreased amplitude

9. It has been already pointed out that electrons in the bonding M.O's tend to pull the nuclei together and that the electrons in the antibonding M.O's tend to separate them. Hence the combined influence of bonding and antibonding electrons may either stabilize or destabilize the molecule, depending on the relative number of these two types of electrons. The stabilizing power is expressed in terms of what is called the "bond order".

$$\text{Bond order} = \frac{1}{2}\left[\left(\begin{array}{c}\text{number of electrons}\\ \text{in the bonding M.O.}\end{array}\right) - \left(\begin{array}{c}\text{number of electrons}\\ \text{in the antibonding M.O.}\end{array}\right)\right]$$

   The greater the bond order, the greater the bond stability and the shorter the bond distance.

10. The M.O's are also named on symmetry grounds. For **homonuclear diatomic molecules**, the symbols 'g' ('gerade' meaning 'even') and 'u' ('ungerade' meaning 'uneven' or 'odd') are used. The symbol 'g' is used, if the orbital has a centre of symmetry. i.e., if along any straight line passing through the centre (This is called the centre of inversion), at equal distances from it, the electron densities are equal and the orbital signs are the same (i.e., the wave function has the same amplitude and sign at the two points which are opposite and equidistant from the centre). If the electron densities are equal, but the orbital signs are opposite at the two points mentioned above, the symbol 'u' is used.

    In the 'σ' type of orbitals, the bonding orbitals are 'g' and the antibonding 'u'; in the 'π' type of orbitals, the bonding orbitals are 'u' and the antibonding 'g'. Figure (a) and (b) below correspond to overlap of 's' orbitals to form 'σ' type of M.O's; Figure (c) and (d) correspond to the formation of 'π' type of M.O's from 'p'-orbitals.

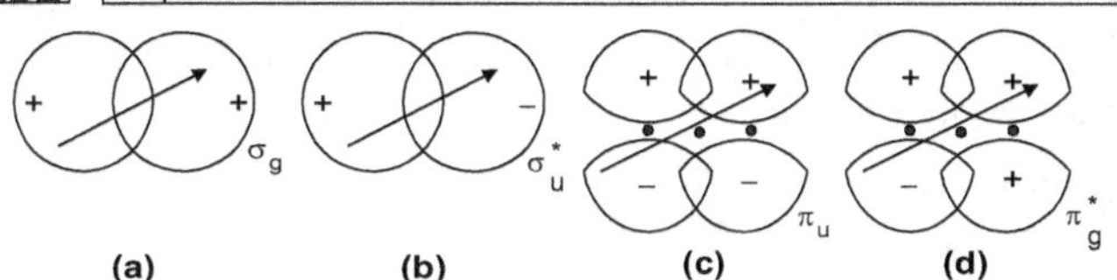

The equivalence of the different notations used to represent the M.O's is shown for a few cases (the x, y, z subscripts in the case of p-orbitals are dropped).

$\sigma(2s)$ or $2s\sigma$ $\Rightarrow \sigma_g(2s)$ $\qquad$ $\sigma^*(2p)$ or $2p\sigma^*$ $\Rightarrow \sigma_u(2p)$

$\sigma^*(2s)$ or $2s\sigma^*$ $\Rightarrow \sigma_u(2s)$ $\qquad$ $\pi(2p)$ or $2p\pi$ $\Rightarrow \pi_u(2p)$

$\sigma(2p)$ or $2p\sigma$ $\Rightarrow \sigma_g(2p)$ $\qquad$ $\pi^*(2p)$ or $2p\pi^*$ $\Rightarrow \pi_g(2p)$

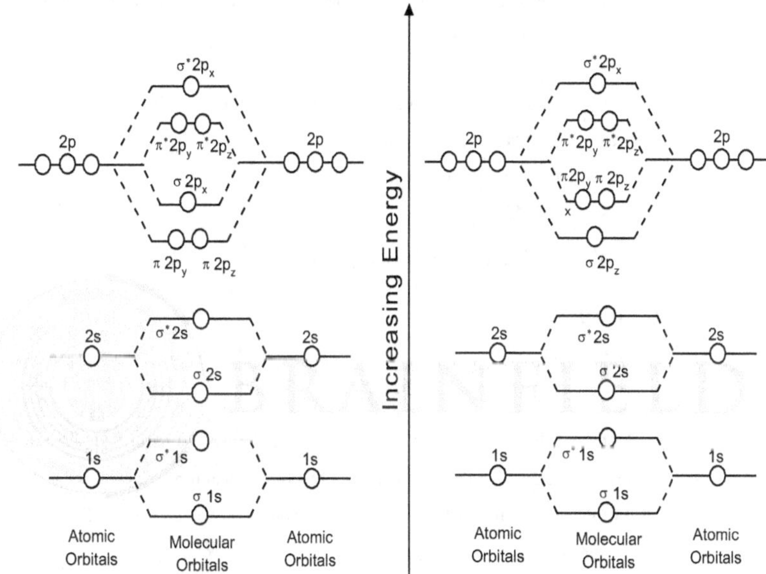

For elements with Z ≤ 7 $\qquad\qquad$ **For elements with Z > 7**

Molecular orbital energy level diagram $\qquad$ **Molecular orbital energy level diagram**

11.1 HOMONUCLEAR DIATOMIC MOLECULES

We shall now consider the electronic configuration of a few homonuclear diatomic molecules.

1. H_2: Electronic configuration of H atom: $1s^1$.

$\therefore$ in H_2 molecule there are 2 electrons. M.O. configuration of H_2 is $\sigma 1s^2$. There is no electron in antibonding M.O. $\therefore$ Bond order (B.O.) $= \dfrac{2-0}{2} = 1$

2. He_2: Electronic configuration of He atom: $1s^2$

$\therefore$ in He_2 molecule there are 4 electrons. The M.O. configuration for He is $\sigma 1s^2$, σ^*1s^2.

$\therefore$ Bond order $= \dfrac{2-2}{2} = 0$.

$\therefore$ He_2 molecule is not stable.

Taking He_2^+, the structure is $\sigma 1s^2$, σ^*1s^1.

$$\therefore \text{B.O.} = \frac{2-1}{2} = \frac{1}{2}.$$

$\therefore$ He_2^+ is stabler than He_2.

3. Li_2: (Li atom: $1s^2\,2s^1$). Total number of electrons in $Li_2 = 6$. Molecular orbital configuration of Li_2 is $\sigma 1s^2$, σ^*1s^2, $\sigma 2s^2$, σ^*2s^0 or [KK] $\sigma 2s^2$, σ^*2s^0.

where KK corresponds to filled $\sigma(1s)$ and $\sigma^*(1s)$ levels. The contribution of [KK] to bond order is zero. Therefore, we can ignore it and consider only the valence electrons.

$$\text{B.O.} = \frac{2-0}{2} = 1$$

$\therefore$ Li_2 is stable and it is found to exist to some extent in lithium vapour.

4. Be_2: (Be: $1s^2 2s^2$)

Molecular orbital structure of Be_2 is:

[KK] $\sigma 2s^2$, σ^*2s^2. Ignoring [KK],

$$\text{B.O.} = \frac{2-2}{2} = 0. \quad \therefore Be_2 \text{ is not stable.}$$

5. B_2: (B: $1s^2\,2s^2\,2p^1$)

M.O. structure of B_2 is

[KK] $\sigma 2s^2$, σ^*2s^2, $\pi 2p_y^1$, $\pi 2p_z^1$.

Note that though $\pi(2p)$ orbital is usually more energetic than $\sigma(2p)$, there is an inversion of the order here due to mixing (hybridization) of $\sigma(2s)$ and $\sigma(2p)$ orbitals. Also note that the degenerate M.O's $\pi(2p_y)$ and $\pi((2p_z)$ have one electron in each according to Hund's principle.

$$\text{B.O.} = \frac{4-2}{2} = 1$$

$\therefore$ B_2 is stable.

Since there are two unpaired electrons in the molecule, B_2 is paramagnetic.

6. C_2: (C: $1s^2\,2s^2\,2p^2$).

M.O. picture of C_2 is:

[KK] $\sigma 2s^2$, σ^*2s^2, $\pi 2p_y^2$, $\pi 2p_z^2$

Here again $\pi(2p)$ orbital is less energetic than $\sigma(2p)$.

$$\text{B.O.} = \frac{6-2}{2} = 2 \text{ and the molecule is stable.}$$

Since there is no unpaired electron, C_2 is diamagnetic. [If $\pi(p)$ orbital had been more energetic than $\sigma(p)$, C_2 would have been paramagnetic, which is contrary to experimental observation.]

7. N_2: (N: $1s^2 2s^2 2p^3$).

M.O. picture of N_2 is:

$[KK]\ \sigma\,2s^2,\ \sigma^*\,2s^2,\ \pi\,2p_y^2,\ \pi\,2p_z^2,\ \sigma\,2p_x^2$

Ignoring the subscripts x, y and z for the p-orbital and considering, only valence electrons, the representation is $\{\sigma(2s)\}^2\ \{\sigma^*(2s)\}^2\ \{\pi(2p)^4\ \{\sigma(2p)\}^2$.

$$B.O. = \frac{8-2}{2} = 3$$

The molecule is diamagnetic. For N_2^+, $B.O. = \dfrac{7-2}{2} = 2.5$.

8. O_2: $[O:\ 1s^2 2s^2\ 2p^4]$

M.O. structure of O_2 is:

$[KK]\ \sigma 2s^2,\ \sigma^* 2s^2,\ \sigma 2p_x^2,\ \pi 2p_y^2,\ \pi 2p_z^2,\ \pi^* 2p_y^1,\ \pi^* 2p_z^1$

$$B.O. = \frac{8-4}{2} = 2$$

Due to the presence of unpaired electrons in the two antibonding orbitals (Hund's rule), O_2 is paramagnetic. The M.O. theory here is superior to the V.B. theory, which does not explain the paramagnetic behaviour of O_2.

Let us now compare the bond strengths of O_2, O_2^+, O_2^-, O_2^{2-}. For O_2, $B.O. = 2$.

For O_2^+: one electron from the antibonding M.O. has been removed.

$$\therefore\ B.O. = \frac{8-3}{2} = 2.5$$

For O_2^-: one electron is added to the antibonding M.O.

$$\therefore\ B.O. = \frac{8-5}{2} = 1.5$$

For O_2^{2-}: $B.O. = \dfrac{8-6}{2} = 1$

$\therefore$ the bond is strongest in O_2^+ and the bond length the least.

PROFICIENCY TEST– II

The following 10 questions deal with the basic concepts of this section. Answer the following briefly. Go to the next section only if your score is greater than or equal to 8.
Do not consult the study material while attempting the questions.

1. True/False.   In PCl_5, all bonds are equivalent and have same bond length.

2. True/False.   Sigma bonds are stronger than pi–bonds.

3. True/False.   The hybridization of the central atom in SO_2 in sp^2.

4. True/False. H_2O forms the strongest intermolecular hydrogen bond.

5. True/False.   The bond strength of O–O bond is more in O_2^+ then in O_2^-.

6. The shape of SF_4 is _____________.

7. A molecule of acetylene has _____________ sigma and _____________ pi–bonds.

8. The hybridization of Cl in ClO^- and ClO_4^- is _____________ and _____________ respectively.

9. o–hydroxy benzaldehyde is _____________ volatile than p–hydroxy benzaldehyde.

10. When NO is converted to NO^+, bond length of N–O bond _____________ while when CN is converted to CN^+, bond length of C–N bond _____________.

ANSWERS TO PROFICIENCY TEST– II

1. False

2. True

3. True

4. False

5. True

6. See–saw shaped or irregular tetrahedron.

7. 3, 2

8. sp^3 in both

9. More

10. Decreases, increases

MIND MAP

CHEMICAL BONDING

1. Atoms combine in order to achieve a more stable (Noble gas) configuration. A covalently bonded molecule can be represented by Lewis structure, which shows bonding and non–bonding electron pairs.

2. According to VSEPR model, molecular geometry can be predicted from the number of bonding electron pairs and lone pairs. It is based on the assumption that valence shell electron pairs repel one another and tend to stay as far apart as possible.

3. Hybridization is the process of mixing up of two or more orbitals to form an equivalent number of orbitals having the same shape and energy. Common hybridizations are: sp, sp^2, sp^3, sp^3d, sp^3d^2 etc.

4. Dipole moment is a measure of the charge separation in molecules containing atoms of different electronegativities. The dipole moment of a molecule is the resultant of whatever bond moments are present.

5. Hydrogen bond is a bond formed between hydrogen and a highly electronegative element like N, O or F, either of the same molecule or of a different molecule but to which the hydrogen is not directly bonded by a covalent bond and the hydrogen itself should be bonded to a highly electronegative element like N, O or F.

(i) Intermolecular: Between two molecules. Increases boiling point.

(ii) Intramolecular: Within a molecule. Decreases boiling point.

6. Molecular orbital theory describes bonding in terms of the combination and rearrangement of atomic orbitals to form orbitals that are associated with the molecule as a whole. Molecules are stable if the number of electrons in bonding molecular orbitals is greater than that in antibonding molecular orbitals.

SOLVED OBJECTIVE EXAMPLES

Example 1:

Which of the following molecules is linear?

(a) ICl   (b) SO_3

(c) O_3 (d) SO_2

Solution:

A diatomic molecule is always linear. So, option (a) is definitely correct. For more than one correct answer questions one would require to check all the options. SO_3 is triangular planar, O_3 and SO_2 are bent.

$\therefore$ (a)

Example 2:

Which of the following hydride is ionic?

(a) H_2O (b) NH_3

(c) CaH_2 (d) H_2S

Solution:

Metallic hydrides are ionic while non–metallic hydrides are covalent.

$\therefore$ (c)

Example 3:

A covalent molecule AB$_4$ (not a complex) will have which of the following hybridisation if it is square planar.

(a) sp^3 (b) sp^3d

(c) sp^3d^2 (d) dsp^2

Solution:

A covalent non–complex molecule does not form dsp^2 hybridization. AB_4 with sp^3 hybridization is tetrahedral, with sp^3d is T–shaped, with sp^3d^2 is square planar.

$\therefore$ (c)

Example 4:

How many types of bond lengths are there in SO_4^{2-}?

(a) one   (b) two

(c) three   (d) four

Solution:

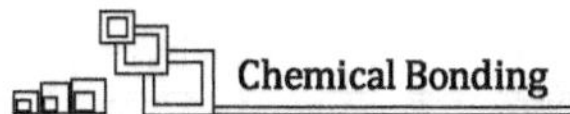

Due to resonance all bond length are same.

$\therefore$ (a)

Example 5:

A molecule XY$_2$ contains two σ, two π–bonds and one lone pair in valence shell of X. The arrangement of lone pair as well as bond pair is

(a) square pyramidal   (b) linear

(c) trigonal planar   (d) unpredictable

Solution:

There are a total of three bond and lone pairs. The best possible arrangement for this is trigonal planar.

$\therefore$ (c)

SOLVED SUBJECTIVE EXAMPLES

Example 1:

Why does CS_2 have zero dipole moment while H_2S does not?

Solution:

CS_2 is linear and symmetrical, while H_2S is bent.

Example 2:

Why C_2H_2 is more acidic than C_2H_6 although the bond energy of C–H bond in C_2H_2 is more than in C_2H_6?

Solution:

Acidic strength involves heterolytic cleavage while bond energy measures the energy for breaking a bond homolytically. In C_2H_2, 'C' is sp hybridized and so is more electronegative than C in C_2H_6 which is sp^3 hybridized.

Example 3:

Why is H_2^+ more stable than H_2^- even though both have equal bond order?

Solution:

H_2^+ has less antibonding electron (zero) while H_2^- has more antibonding electron (one).

Example 4:

CuCl is more covalent than NaCl even though both Cu^+ and Na^+ have the same size. Why?

Solution:

Cu^+ has more nuclear charge.

Example 5:

Why is oxygen atom in $XeOF_2$ in equatorial plane?

Solution:

Out of the surrounding atoms the least electronegative atom behaves like a lone pair.

EXERCISE – I

JEE & NEET-SINGLE CHOICE CORRECT

1. PCl_5 exists but NCl_5 does not because
   (a) nitrogen has no vacant d–orbitals
   (b) NCl_5 in unstable
   (c) nitrogen atom is much smaller
   (d) nitrogen is highly inert

2. If a molecule MX_3 has zero dipole moment, the sigma bonding orbitals used by M (atomic number < 21) are
   (a) pure p
   (b) sp hybridised
   (c) sp^2 hybridised
   (d) sp^3 hybridised

3. Of the three molecules XeF_4, SF_4, SiF_4 one which has/have tetrahedral structures is/are
   (a) all the three
   (b) only SiF_4
   (c) both SF_4 and XeF_4
   (d) both SiF_4 and XeF_4

4. The shape of PCl_4^+ ion would be
   (a) square planar
   (b) tetrahedral
   (c) irregular tetrahedron
   (d) square pyramidal

5. Strongest bond is formed by the head on overlapping of
   (a) 2s and 2p–orbitals
   (b) 2p and 2p–orbitals
   (c) 2s and 2s–orbitals
   (d) all of these

6. The hydrogen halide having maximum dipole moment is
   (a) HF
   (b) HCl
   (c) HBr
   (d) HI

7. The state of hybridization of Xe in XeF_4 is
   (a) sp^2
   (b) sp^3
   (c) sp^3d
   (d) sp^3d^2

8. Where is the negative formal charge located in cyanide ion?
   (a) C
   (b) N
   (c) Any of them
   (d) Resonates between C and N

9. Dipole moment is exhibited by
   (a) 1,4 Dichlorobenzene
   (b) 1,2–Dichlorobenzene
   (c) trans–1,2–dichloroethene
   (d) none of these

10. In the following molecule, $H_3C–\overset{*}{C}\equiv\overset{*}{C}–CH_3$ the two carbon atoms marked by asterisk (*) possess the following type of hybridized orbitals
    (a) sp^3–orbital
    (b) sp^2–orbital
    (c) sp–orbital
    (d) s–orbital

11. The pair of species having identical shape is
    (a) CF_4, SF_4
    (b) PCl_3, BF_3
    (c) XeF_2, CO_2
    (d) PF_5, IF_5

12. Shape of ICl_2^- is
    (a) Trigonal
    (b) linear
    (c) Octahedral
    (d) Square planar

13. The species having octahedral shape is
    (a) SF_6
    (b) BF_4^-
    (c) PCl_5
    (d) BO_3^{3-}

14. How many unpaired electrons are present in N_2^+?
    (a) 1
    (b) 2
    (c) 3
    (d) 4

15. Which of the following has fractional bond order?
    (a) O_2^{2+}
    (b) O_2^{2-}
    (c) F_2^{2-}
    (d) H_2^-

16. Among the following compounds, which has the maximum number of sp-hybridized C atoms?
    (a) $(CN)_2$
    (b) $CH_2=C=CH-CN$
    (c) $HC\equiv C-CH_2CH=CH_2$
    (d) $HC\equiv C-CN$

17. According to Fajans' rules, ionic bonds are formed when
    (a) cations have low positive charge and large size.
    (b) cations have low positive charge and small size.
    (c) cations have high positive charge and large size, and anions have a small size.
    (d) cations have a low positive charge and large size, and anions have a small size.

18. What conclusions can we draw from the following reactions?
    $$H_2 + 4.5\,eV \longrightarrow H + H$$
    $$H + 13.6\,eV \longrightarrow H^+ + e^-$$
    (a) It is more difficult to break up an H_2 molecule than it is to ionize a hydrogen atom.
    (b) It is easier to break up an H_2 molecule than it is to ionize a hydrogen atom.
    (c) The average energy of formation of H and H^+ are the same.
    (d) Electron and proton attraction in an H_2 molecule as well as a H atom are the same.

19. In an H_2^+ ion
    (a) one electron is bound to two protons.
    (b) two electrons are bound to two protons.
    (c) three electrons are bound to two protons.
    (d) none of these happens.

20. $AlCl_3$ is covalent while AlF_3 is ionic. This can be justified on the basis of
    (a) the valence-bond theory
    (b) Fajan's rules
    (c) the molecular-orbital theory
    (d) hydration energy

21. Among of the following molecules, which is the most ionic?
    (a) $CaCl_2$
    (b) $SnCl_2$
    (c) $NaCl$
    (d) $CuCl$

22. Among the following, the molecule with the highest dipole moment is
    (a) CH_3Cl
    (b) CH_2Cl_2
    (c) $CHCl_3$
    (d) CCl_4

23. Orthonitrophenol is steam volatile but paranitrophenol is not because
    (a) orthonitrophenol has intramolecular hydrogen bonding while paranitrophenol has intermolecular hydrogen bonding.
    (b) both ortho- and paranitrophenol have intramolecular hydrogen bonding.
    (c) orthonitrophenol has intermolecular hydrogen bonding and paranitrophenol has intramolecular hydrogen bonding.
    (d) Vander Waals forces are dominant in orthonitrophenol.

24. The shape of PCl_4^+, PCl_4^- and $AsCl_5$ are respectively
    (a) square planar, tetrahedral and see-saw
    (b) tetrahedral, see-saw and trigonal bipyramidal
    (c) tetrahedral, square planar and pentagonal bipyramidal
    (d) trigonal bipyramidal, tetrahedral and square pyramidal

25. Which of the following pairs are isostructural?
    (a) CH_3^- and CH_3^+
    (b) NH_4^+ and NH_3
    (c) SO_4^{2-} and BF_4^-
    (d) NH_2^- and BeF_2

EXERCISE – II

IIT-JEE & NEET- SINGLE CHOICE CORRECT

1. The correct order of dipole moment is
(a) $CH_4 < NF_3 < NH_3 < H_2O$
(b) $NF_3 < CH_4 < NH_3 < H_2O$
(c) $NH_3 < NF_3 < CH_4 < H_2O$
(d) $H_2O < NH_3 < NF_3 < CH_4$

2. Carbon atoms in $C_2(CN)_4$ are
(a) sp–hybridised
(b) sp^2–hybridised
(c) sp– and sp^2–hybridised
(d) sp, sp^2 and sp^3–hybridised

3. Which of the following is paramagnetic?
(a) O_2^-
(b) CN^-
(c) CO
(d) NO^+

4. Which of the molecule is T–shaped?
(a) BeF_2
(b) BCl_3
(c) NH_3
(d) CIF_3

5. Which shows a change in the type of hybridization when
(a) NH_3 combines with H^+
(b) AlH_3 combines with H^-
(c) In both cases
(d) In none cases

6. Molecular shapes of SF_4, CF_4 and XeF_4 are
(a) the same, with 2, 0 and 1 lone pair of electrons on central atom, respectively.
(b) the same, with 1, 1 and 1 lone pair of electrons on central atom, respectively.
(c) different, with 0, 1 and 2 lone pair of electrons on central atom, respectively.
(d) different with 1, 0 and 2 lone pair of electrons on central atom, respectively.

7. The hybridization of atomic orbitals of nitrogen in NO_2^+, NO_3^- and NH_4^+ are
(a) sp, sp^3 and sp^2 respectively
(b) sp, sp^2 and sp^3 respectively
(c) sp^2, sp and sp^3 respectively
(d) sp^2, sp^3 and sp respectively

8. Which of the following contains both polar and non–polar bonds?
(a) NH_4Cl
(b) HCN
(c) H_2O_2
(d) CH_4

9. The bond order of the superoxide (O_2^-) is
(a) 1
(b) 1.5
(c) 2
(d) 2.5

10. Amongst LiCl, $BeCl_2$, $MgCl_2$ and RbCl the compounds with greatest and least ionic character, respectively are
(a) LiCl and RbCl
(b) RbCl and $BeCl_2$
(c) RbCl and $MgCl_2$
(d) $MgCl_2$ and $BeCl_2$

11. In which molecule sulphur atom is not sp^3–hybridised
(a) SO_4^{2-}
(b) SF_4
(c) SF_2
(d) S_8

12. Which of the following orders regarding the bond order is correct?
(a) $O_2^- > O_2 > O_2^+$
(b) $O_2^- < O_2 < O_2^+$
(c) $O_2^- > O_2 < O_2^+$
(d) $O_2^- < O_2 > O_2^+$

13. The shape of XeF_4 is
(a) tetrahedral
(b) square planar
(c) pyramidal
(d) nearly linear

14. The shape of $XeOF_4$ is
(a) square pyramidal
(b) square antiprismatic
(c) distorted octahedral
(d) pentagonal bipyramidal

15. The geometry of XeO_2F_2 is
(a) plane triangular
(b) see–saw
(c) square planar
(d) tetrahedral

16. The Xe atom in $XeOF_4$ involves the hybridization
(a) sp^3
(b) sp^3d
(c) sp^3d^2
(d) sp^3d^3

17. The hybridisation of P in PO_4^{3-} is same as that of
(a) I in ICl_4^-
(b) S in SO_3
(c) N in NO_3^-
(d) S in SO_4^{2-}

18. Which of the following statement is correct?
(a) Polarisation of an anion is maximum by high charged cation.
(b) Small sized cation minimizes the polarisation.
(c) A small anion brings about a large degree of polarisation.
(d) A large anion undergoes a small degree of polarisation.

19. Which of the following have identical bond order :
(i) CN^- (ii) O_2^- (iii) NO^+ (iv) CN^+
(a) (i) and (iii)
(b) (ii) and (iv)
(c) (i) and (iv)
(d) (ii) and (iii)

20. Which of the following has highest ionic character?
(a) $MgCl_2$
(b) $CaCl_2$
(c) $BaCl_2$
(d) $BeCl_2$

ONE OR MORE THAN ONE CHOICE CORRECT

1. PCl_3 and PCl_5 both exist but only PH_3 exists while PH_5 does not exist. This is because
(a) H is nearly as electronegative as P.
(b) the activation energy for the formation of PH_5 is very high.
(c) PH_5 immediately decomposes to PH_3 and H_2 because its equilibrium constant for the decomposition is very high.
(d) An element is able to utilize its d–orbitals for bonding only with elements which are more electronegative than it.

2. Which of the following molecules or ions is not linear?
(a) $BeCl_2$
(b) ICl_2^-
(c) CS_2
(d) ICl_2^+

3. Which of the following is/are non–polar but contain(s) polar bonds?
(a) HCl
(b) H_2O
(c) SO_3
(d) CO_2

4. The 90° angles between bond pair–bond pair of electrons exists in
(a) ClF_3
(b) I_3^-
(c) BrF_5
(d) PCl_4^+

5. Which of the following species is paramagnetic?

   (a) CN^-

   (b) NO

   (c) O_2^{2-}

   (d) O_2

6. Shape of I_3^- is

   (a) tetrahedral

   (b) triangular bipyramidal

   (c) distorted trigonal bipyramidal

   (d) linear

7. Which among the following has bond order zero?

   (a) F_2^{2-}

   (b) Ar_2

   (c) He_2^{+1}

   (d) H_2^{+1}

8. KF combines with HF to form KHF_2. The compound contains the species

   (a) K^+, F^- and H^+

   (b) K^+, F^- and HF

   (c) K^+ and $[HF_2]^-$

   (d) one cation and one anion

9. Among the following species, identify the isostructural pairs

   NF_3, NO_3^-, BF_3, H_3O^+, N_3^-, I_3^-

   (a) $[NF_3, NO_3^-]$ and $[BF_3, H_3O^+]$

   (b) $[I_3^-, N_3^-]$ and $[NO_3^-, BF_3]$

   (c) $[NF_3, H_3O^+]$ and $[NO_3^-, BF_3]$

   (d) $[NF_3, H_3O^+]$ and $[N_3^-, I_3^-]$

10. NH_3 and BF_3 form adduct readily

    (a) Hybridization of NH_3 remains same.

    (b) through co–ordinate bond between B and N

    (c) Hybridization of NH_3 changes from sp^3 to sp^2.

    (d) Hybridization of B changes from sp^2 to sp^3.

EXERCISE – III

MATCH THE FOLLOWING

1.

Column I (Compounds)	Column II (Shape / Property)
I. CH_4	**(A)** tetrahedral
II. NH_3	**(B)** hydrogen bonding
III. HF	**(C)** see–saw
IV. SF_4	**(D)** linear
	(E) polar molecule

REASONING TYPE

Directions: Read the following questions and choose
- **(A) If both the statements are true and statement-2 is the correct explanation of statement-1.**
- **(B) If both the statements are true but statement-2 is not the correct explanation of statement-1.**
- **(C) If statement-1 is True and statement-2 is False.**
- **(D) If statement-1 is False and statement-2 is True.**

1. **Statement-1:** Xe atom in XeF_2 assumes sp hybrid state.
   Statement-2: XeF_2 molecule does not follow octet rule.
   (a) (A)   (b) (B)   (c) (C)   (d) (D)

2. **Statement-1:** NO_2 is paramagnetic at room temperature and diamagnetic at lower temperature.
   Statement-2: When electrons are odd, the molecule is paramagnetic or else diamagnetic.
   (a) (A)   (b) (B)   (c) (C)   (d) (D)

3. **Statement-1:** SO_2 is bent.
   Statement-2: SO_2 has two π bonds.
   (a) (A)   (b) (B)   (c) (C)   (d) (D)

4. **Statement-1:** Bond angle of NH_3 is lower than in CH_4.
   Statement-2: NH_3 has one lone pair and lone pair–bond pair repulsion is greater than bond pair–bond pair repulsion.
   (a) (A)   (b) (B)   (c) (C)   (d) (D)

5. **Statement-1:** H_2O is liquid while H_2S is gas.
   Statement-2: H_2O has hydrogen bonding while H_2S does not.
   (a) (A)   (b) (B)   (c) (C)   (d) (D)

LINKED COMPREHENSION TYPE

Ionic bond is defined as the electrostatic force of attraction holding the oppositely charged ions. Ionic compounds are mostly crystalline solids having high melting and boiling points, electrical conductivity in molten state, solubility in water etc. Covalent bond is defined as the force which binds atoms of same or different elements by mutual sharing of electrons in a covalent bond. Covalent compounds are solids, liquids or gases. They are low melting and boiling point compounds. They are more soluble in non–polar solvents.

1. The valence electrons not involved in formation of covalent bonds are called
   (a) non–bonding electrons
   (b) lone pairs
   (c) unshared pairs
   (d) all of these

2. The amount of energy released when one mole of ionic solid is formed by close packing of gaseous ion is called:
   (a) Ionisation energy
   (b) Solvation energy
   (c) Lattice energy
   (d) Hydration energy

3. Which of the following gives a white precipitate with $AgNO_3$?
   (a) NaCl
   (b) CCl_4
   (c) CO_2
   (d) $CHCl_3$

EXERCISE – IV

SUBJECTIVE PROBLEMS

1. $MgCl_2$ is linear but $SnCl_2$ is angular. Explain.
2. Although I_3^- is known, F_3^- is not. Why?
3. Why are inert gases less reactive?
4. Predict the shapes of the following molecules using the VSEPR model : $BeCl_2$, $SiCl_4$, AsF_5, H_2S, PH_3.
5. Dichlorobenzene exists in three different isomers called ortho, meta and para. Which of these would have a non zero dipole moment and why?
6. Account for the fact that carbon–carbon bond lengths in ethane, ethene and ethyne are 154 pm, 134 pm and 120 pm, respectively.
7. On what factors does the polarity of a molecule depend?
8. Why is bond energy of P–Cl bond different in PCl_3 and PCl_5?
9. The hybridisation of central atom in CH_4, H_2O and NH_3 is sp^3. Why are the bond angles different in these three cases?
10. BF_3 and graphite, both are coplanar having sp^2 hybridization but later is a conductor. Explain.
11. XeF_2 is linear inspite of the fact that Xe involves sp^3d hybridisation. Explain.
12. Give reason why ClF_3 exists but FCl_3 does not?
13. $NaCl_{aq.}$ gives a white precipitate with $AgNO_3$ solution but CCl_4 or $CHCl_3$ does not. Explain.
14. Explain why N_2 has greater dissociation energy than N_2^+.
15. $BaSO_4$ being an electrovalent compound does not pass into solution state in water. Explain.

ANSWERS

EXERCISE – I

IIT & NEET-SINGLE CHOICE CORRECT

1. (a)	2. (c)	3. (b)	4. (b)	5. (b)
6. (a)	7. (d)	8. (d)	9. (b)	10. (c)
11. (c)	12. (b)	13. (a)	14. (a)	15. (d)
16. (d)	17. (d)	18. (b)	19. (a)	20. (b)
21. (c)	22. (a)	23. (a)	24. (b)	25. (c)

EXERCISE – II

IIT-JEE-SINGLE CHOICE CORRECT

1. (a)	2. (c)	3. (a)	4. (d)	5. (b)
6. (d)	7. (b)	8. (c)	9. (b)	10. (b)
11. (b)	12. (b)	13. (b)	14. (a)	15. (b)
16. (c)	17. (d)	18. (a)	19. (a)	20. (c)

ONE OR MORE THAN ONE CHOICE CORRECT

1. (a, d)	2. (d)	3. (c, d)	4. (a, c)	5. (b, d)
6. (c, d)	7. (a, b)	8. (c, d)	9. (b, c, d)	10. (a, b, d)

EXERCISE – III

MATCH THE FOLLOWING

1.   I – (A) ; II – (B), (E) ; III – (B), (D), (E) ; IV – (C), (E)

REASONING TYPE

1. (d)	2. (c)	3. (b)	4. (a)	5. (a)

LINKED COMPREHENSION TYPE

1. (d)	2. (c)	3. (a)

EXERCISE – IV

SUBJECTIVE PROBLEMS

1. $MgCl_2$ is sp hybridized, whereas $SnCl_2$ is sp^2 hybridized.
2. Iodine can expand its octet due to presence of vacant d-orbitals while F cannot.
3. Inert gases have fully filled ns^2np^6 configuration of valence shell.
4. $BeCl_2$: linear ; $SiCl_4$; tetrahedral ; AsF_5 : trigonal bipyramidal ; H_2S : angular ; PH_3 : pyramidal
5. Ortho and meta dichlorobenzene have got a non zero dipole moment because of unsymmetrical structure.
6. Ethane, ethene and ethyne contain single, double and triple bond respectively and bond length is inversely related to bond order.
7. The molecule contains polar bonds and must be non symmetrical in nature.
8. Phosphorus atom is sp^3 hybridised in PCl_3 and sp^3d hybridised in PCl_5.
9. Bond angles of CH_4, H_2O and NH_3 are different due to presence of one and two lone pairs on N in NH_3 and O in H_2O respectively while CH_4 has no lone pair.
10. Graphite (C) has one unhybridized p-orbital containing single electron. Due to this free electron, graphite is used as a conductor.
11. In XeF_2 molecules, out of five sp^3d hybridised orbitals, the three equatorial orbitals have one lone pair each while the two axial orbitals have one bond pair each. This results in linear shape of XeF_2.
12. Chlorine can expand its octet due to the presence of vacant d–orbitals.
13. NaCl is an ionic compound while CCl_4 and $CHCl_3$ are covalent. NaCl gives Na^+ and Cl^- in aqueous solution.
14. In N_2 molecule, bond order is three. In N_2^+ one electron is removed from bonding molecular orbital $(\sigma 2p_x)$. This reduces the bond order to 2.5. Since bond order is directly proportional to bond strength, N_2 has higher dissociation energy than N_2^+.
15. The lattice energy of $BaSO_4$ is more than the hydration energy.

Single Correct Answer Type

1. Born-Haber cycle may be used to calculate
   1) Electronegativity
   2) Mass number
   3) Oxidation number
   4) Electron affinity

2. Value of x in potash alum,
   $K_2SO_4 . Al_x(SO_4)_3 . 24H_2O$ is
   1) 4
   2) 1
   3) 2
   4) None of these

3. Which of the following is a favourable factor for cation formation?
   1) Low ionisation potential
   2) High electron affinity
   3) High electronegativity
   4) Small atomic size

4. If Na^+ ion is larger than Mg^{2+} ion and S^{2-} is larger than Cl^- ion, which of the following will be stable soluble in water?
   1) Sodium chloride
   2) Sodium sulphide
   3) Magnesium chloride
   4) Magnesium sulphide

5. Which of the following is not correct regarding the properties of ionic compounds?
   1) Ionic compounds have high metling and boiling points
   2) Their reaction velocity in aqueous medium is very high
   3) Ionic compounds in their molten and aqueous solutions do not conduct electricity
   4) They are highly soluble in polar solvents

6. Which of the following has minimum melting point?
   1) CsF
   2) HCl
   3) HF
   4) LiF

7. Oxidising power of chlorine in aqueous solution can be determined by the parameters indicated below

   $$\frac{1}{2}Cl_2(g) \xrightarrow{\frac{1}{2}\Lambda_{diss}H^o} Cl(g) \xrightarrow{\Lambda_{EA}H^o} Cl^-(g) \xrightarrow{\Delta_{hyd}H^o} Cl^-(aq)$$

   The energy involved in the conversion of $\frac{1}{2}Cl_2(g)$ to $Cl^-(aq)$ (Using the data)

   $\Delta_{diss}H^o_{Cl_2} = 240$ kJmol^{-1}

   $\Delta_{EA}H^o_{Cl} = -349$ kJmol^{-1}

   $\Delta_{hyd}H^o Cl = -381$ kJmol^{-1} will be
   1) $+152$ kJmol^{-1}
   2) -610 kJmol^{-1}
   3) -850 kJmol^{-1}
   4) $+120$ kJmol^{-1}

8. In the following electron-dot structure, calculate the formal charge from left to right nitrogen atom;

   $$\ddot{N} = N = \ddot{N}$$

   1) $-1, -1, +1$
   2) $-1, +1, -1$
   3) $+1, -1, -1$
   4) $+1, -1, +1$

9. The number of electrons in the valence shell of sulphur in SF_6 is
   1) 12
   2) 10
   3) 8
   4) 11

10. Which of the following is a favourable factor for cation formation?
    1) High electronegativity
    2) High electron affinity
    3) Low ionisation potential
    4) Smaller atomic size

11. Which one of the following has a coordinate bond?
    1) NH_4Cl 2) $AlCl_3$
    3) NaCl   4) Cl_2

12. The electronic theory of bonding was proposed by
    1) Pauling   2) Lewis
    3) Bronsted   4) Mullikan

13. The lattice enthalpy and hydration enthalpy of four compounds are given below.

Compound	Lattice enthalpy (in kJ mol^{-1})	Hydration enthalpy (in kJ mol^{-1})
P	+780	-920
Q	+1012	-812
R	+828	-878
S	+632	-600

The pair of compounds which is soluble in water is
    1) P and Q 2) Q and R
    3) R and S 4) Q and S
    5) P and R

14. Which type of bond is present in H_2S molecule?
    1) Ionic bond   2) Covalent bond
    3) Coordinate   4) All of three

15. When a metal atom combines with a non-metal atom, the non-metal atom will
    1) Lose electrons and decrease in size   2) Lose electrons and increase in size
    3) Gain electrons and decrease in size   4) Gain electrons and increase in size

16. An atom of an element A has three electrons in its outermost orbit and that of B has six electrons in its outermost orbit. The formula of the compound between these two will be
    1) A_3B_6 2) A_2B_3
    3) A_3B_2 4) A_2B

17. During the formation of a chemical bond
    1) Electron-electron repulsion becomes more than the nucleus-electron repulsion attraction   2) Energy of the system does not change
    3) Energy increases   4) Energy decreases

18. Consider the Born-Haber cycle for the formation of an ionic compound given below and identify the compound (Z) formed.

$$\left[\begin{array}{c} M(s) \xrightarrow{\Delta H_1} M(g) \xrightarrow{\Delta H_2} M^+(g) \\ \frac{1}{2}X_2(g) \xrightarrow{\Delta H_3} X(g) \xrightarrow{\Delta H_4} X^-(g) \end{array}\right] \xrightarrow{\Delta H_5} Z$$

    1) M^+X^- 2) $M^+X^-(s)$
    3) MX 4) $M^+X^-(g)$

19. An example of a polar covalent compound is
    1) KCl   2) NaCl
    3) CCl_4 4) HCl
    5) CH_4

20. Which combination of atoms can form a polar covalent bond?
    1) H and H   2) H and Br
    3) N and N   4) Na and Br

21. Lattice energy of an ionic compound depends upon
   1) Charge on the ion and size of the ion
   2) Packing of ions only
   3) Size of the ion only
   4) Charge on the ion only

22. Lattice energy of a solid increases if
   1) Size of ions is small
   2) Charges of ions are small
   3) Ions are neutral
   4) None of the above

23. Which of the following represents the Lewis structure of N_2 molecule?
   1) 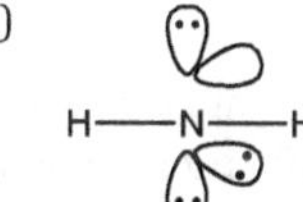
   2)
   3)
   4)

24. The polarising ability of which one of the following is highest?
   1) Small highly positive ion
   2) Large positive ion
   3) Small highly negative ion
   4) Large negative ion

25. The value of n in the molecular formula Be $_nAl_2Si_6O_{18}$ is
   1) 1
   2) 2
   3) 3
   4) 4

26. Among the following the maximum covalent character is shown by the compound.
   1) $FeCl_2$
   2) $SnCl_2$
   3) $AlCl_3$
   4) $MgCl_2$

27. Which one of the following is highest melting halide?
   1) AgCl
   2) AgBr
   3) AgF
   4) AgI

28. Which of the following has lowest boiling point?
   1) NaCl
   2) CuCl
   3) $CuCl_2$
   4) CsCl

29. For $\bar{N}H_2$, the best three-dimensional view is
   1) 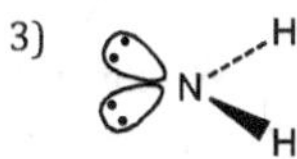
   2) 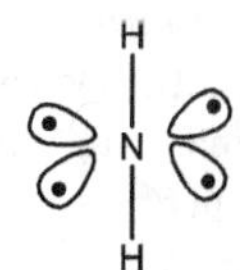
   3)
   4)

30. AB is an ionic solid. The ionic radii of A^+ and B^+ are respectively r_c and r_a. Lattice energy of AB is proportional to
   1) $\dfrac{r_c}{r_a}$
   2) $(r_c + r_a)$
   3) $\dfrac{r_a}{r_c}$
   4) $\dfrac{1}{(r_c + r_a)}$

31. Number of electrons in a the valence orbit of nitrogen in an ammonia molecule is
   1) 8
   2) 5
   3) 6
   4) 7

32. Which metal has a greater tendency to form metal oxide?
    1) Cr
    2) Fe
    3) Al
    4) Ca

33. The number of oxygen atoms bonded to one phosphorus atom in P_4O_6 is
    1) 4
    2) 3
    3) 6
    4) 5

34. Which of the following has covalent bond?
    1) Na_2S
    2) $AlCl_3$
    3) NaH
    4) $MgCl_2$

35. Among the following, the compound that contains ionic, covalent and coordinate linkage is
    1) NH_3
    2) NH_4Cl
    3) $NaCl$
    4) CaO

36. The following salt shows maximum covalent character
    1) $AlCl_3$
    2) $MgCl_2$
    3) $CsCl$
    4) $LaCl_3$

37. Which of the following silver salts is insoluble in water?
    1) $AgClO_4$
    2) Ag_2SO_4
    3) AgF
    4) $AgNO_3$

38. Sodium chloride is soluble in water but not in benzene because
    1) $\Delta H_{\text{hdydration}} < \Delta H_{\text{lattice energy in water}}$ and $\Delta H_{\text{hdydration}} > \Delta H_{\text{lattice energy in benzene}}$
    2) $\Delta H_{\text{hdydration}} > \Delta H_{\text{lattice energy in water}}$ and $\Delta H_{\text{hdydration}} < \Delta H_{\text{lattice energy in benzene}}$
    3) $\Delta H_{\text{hdydration}} = \Delta H_{\text{lattice energy in water}}$ and $\Delta H_{\text{hdydration}} < \Delta H_{\text{lattice energy in benzene}}$
    4) $\Delta H_{\text{Hdydration}} < \Delta H_{\text{lattice energy in water}}$ and $\Delta H_{\text{Hdydration}} = \Delta H_{\text{lattice energy in benzene}}$

39. What is the nature of the bond between B and O in $(C_2H_5)_2OBH_3$?
    1) Covalent
    2) Coordinate covalent
    3) Ionic bond
    4) Banana shaped bond

40. A coordinate bond is a dative covalent bond. Which of the below is true?
    1) Three atom form bond by sharing their electrons
    2) Two atoms form bond by sharing their electrons
    3) Two atoms form bond and one of them provides both electrons
    4) Two atoms form bond by sharing electrons obtained from third atom.

41. Which of the following when dissolved in water forms a solution, *i.e.*, non-conducting?
    1) Chile salt petre
    2) Potash alum
    3) Green vitriol
    4) Ethyl alcohol

42. Carnallite in solution in water shows the properties of
    1) K^+, Mg^{2+}, Cl^-
    2) $K^+, Cl^-, SO_4^{2-}, Br^-$
    3) K^+, Mg^{2+}, CO_3^{2-}
    4) K^+, Mg^{2+}, Cl^-, Br^-

43. Allene (C_3H_4) contains
    1) One double bond, one triple bond and one single bond
    2) One triple and two double bonds
    3) Two triple and one double bond
    4) Two double and four single bond

44. Which one of the following contains both ionic and covalent bonds?
    1) C_6H_5Cl
    2) H_2O
    3) $NaOH$
    4) CO_2

45. A compound contains X, Y and Z atoms. The oxidation states of X, Y and Z are +2, +2 and -2 respectively. The possible formula of the compound is
   1) XYZ_2
   2) $Y_2(XZ_3)_2$
   3) $X_3(Y_4Z)_2$
   4) $X_3(YZ_4)_3$

46. Oxygen and the oxide ion have the
   1) Same proton number
   2) Same electronic configuration
   3) Same electron number
   4) Same size

47. The nature of the bond in diamond is
   1) Ionic
   2) Covalent
   3) Metallic
   4) Coordinate covalent

48. When metals react with non-metals, the metal atoms tend to
   1) Share electrons
   2) Lose electrons
   3) Gain electrons
   4) None of the above

49. The charge/size ratio of a cation determines its polarising power. Which one of the following sequences represents the increasing order of the polarising power of the cationic species, $K^+, Ca^{2+}, Mg^{2+}, Be^{2+}$?
   1) $Mg^{2+} < Be^{2+} < K^+ < Ca^{2+}$
   2) $Be^{2+} < K^+ < Ca^{2+} < Mg^{2+}$
   3) $K^+ < Ca^{2+} < Mg^{2+} < Be^{2+}$
   4) $Ca^{2+} < Mg^{2+} < Be^{2+} < K^+$

50. Which of the following shows minimum melting point?
   1) Naphthalene
   2) Diamond
   3) NaCl
   4) Mn

51. C − Cl bond is stronger than C − I bond, because
   1) C − Cl bond is more ionic than C − I
   2) C − Cl bond is polar covalent bond
   3) C − Cl bond is more covalent than C − I
   4) C − Cl bond length is longer than C − I

52. The bond length of HCl molecule is 1.275 Å and its dipole moment is 1.03 D. The ionic character of the molecule (in per cent) (charge of the electron= 4.8×10^{-10} esu) is
   1) 100
   2) 67.3
   3) 33.66
   4) 16.83

53. Consider the following halogen containing compounds
   (A)$CHCl_3$ (B)
   (C)CH_2Cl_2 (D)
   (E)

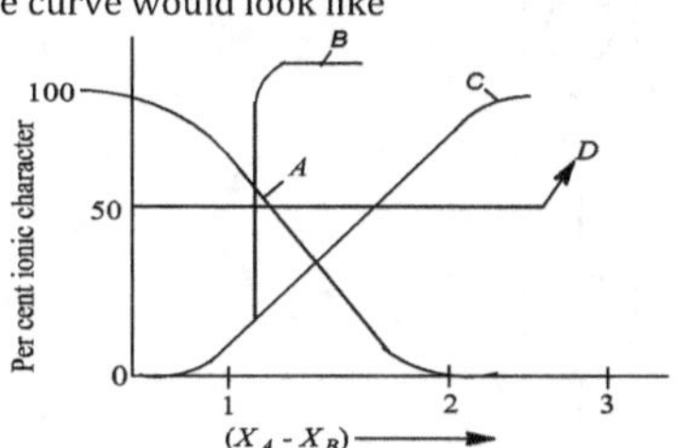

   The compounds with a net zero dipole moment are
   1) B and E only
   2) C only
   3) C and D only
   4) A and D only
   5) B only

54. For AB bond if per cent ionic character is plotted against electronegativity difference $(X_A - X_B)$, the shape of the curve would look like

   The correct curve is
   1) A
   2) B
   3) C
   4) D

55. The molecule which has zero moment is
1) CH_3Cl
2) NF_3
3) BF_3
4) ClO_2

56. If $H - X$ bond length is 2.00 Å and $H - X$ bond has dipole moment $5.12 \times 10^{-30} C - m$, the percentage of ionic character in the molecule will be
1) 10%
2) 16%
3) 18%
4) 20%

57. Dipole moment is shown by
1) *cis*- 1, 2-dichloro ethane
2) *trans*-1, 2-dichloro ethane
3) *trans*-1 2-dichloro-2 peptene
4) Both (a) and (c)

58. The molecule which does not exhibit dipole moment is
1) NH_3
2) $CHCl_3$
3) H_2O
4) CCl_4

59. The dipole moment of HBr is 1.6×10^{-30} cm and inter – atomic spacing is 1 Å. The % ionic character of HBr is
1) 7
2) 10
3) 15
4) 27

60. The molecule having zero dipole moment is
1) CH_2Cl_2
2) BF_3
3) NF_3
4) ClF_3

61. Which one of the following pairs of molecules will have permanent dipole moments for both members?
1) SiF_4 and NO_2
2) NO_2 and CO_2
3) NO_2 and O_3
4) SiF_4 and CO_2

62. Which substance has the greatest ionic character?
1) Cl_2O
2) NCl_3
3) $PbCl_2$
4) $BaCl_2$

63. If the bond length and dipole moment of a diatomic molecule are 1.25 A and 1.0 D respectively, what is the per cent ionic character of the bond?
1) 10.66
2) 12.33
3) 16.66
4) 19.33

64. Which of the following will have large dipole moment?

1) NH_2 (benzene ring)

2) NO_2 (benzene ring)

3) NH_2 (benzene ring with NO_2 para)

4) NH_2 (benzene ring with NO_2 meta)

65. C – C bond order in benzene is
   1) 1
   2) 2
   3) Between 1 and 2
   4) None of these

66. The molecule having largest dipole moment among the following is
   1) CHI_3
   2) CH_4
   3) $CHCl_3$
   4) CCl_4

67. The correct stability order of the following resonance structure is

   $$H_2C = \overset{+}{N} = \overset{-}{N} \qquad H_2C - \overset{+}{N} = \overset{-}{N}$$

   $$H_2\overset{-}{C} - \overset{+}{N} \equiv N$$

   1) (I) > (II) > (IV) > (III)
   2) (I) > (III) > (II) > (IV)
   3) (II) > (I) > (III) > (IV)
   4) (III) > (I) > (IV) > (II)

68. If the molecule of HCl were totally polar, the expected value of dipole moment is 6.12 D (dbye), but the experimental value of dipole moment was 1.03 D. Calculate the percentage ionic character
   1) 17
   2) 83
   3) 50
   4) Zero
   5) 90

69. Zero dipole moment is possessed by
   1) PCl_3
   2) BF_3
   3) ClF_3
   4) NH_3

70. Which of the following are possible resonating structure of N_2O?

   I

   II

   III

   IV

   1) I and II
   2) I and III
   3) I, II and III
   4) All of these

71. Among the following the molecule with the highest dipole moment is
   1) CH_3Cl
   2) CH_2Cl_2
   3) $CHCl_3$
   4) CCl_4

72. Which one of the following is a non-polar molecule?
   1) CCl_4
   2) $CHCl_3$
   3) CH_2Cl_2
   4) CH_3Cl

73. Identify the non-polar molecule in the set of compounds given
   HCl, HF, H_2, HBr
   1) H_2
   2) HCl
   3) HF, HBr
   4) HBr

74. The bond angle and dipole moment of water respectively, are
   1) 109.5°, 1.84 D
   2) 107.5°, 1.56 D
   3) 104.5°, 1.84 D
   4) 102.5°, 1.56 D

75. In the anion $HCOO^-$ the two carbon-oxygen bonds are found to be of equal length. What is the reason for it?

1) Electronic orbits of carbon atom are hybridised
2) The C=O bond is weaker than the $C-O$ bond
3) The anion $HCOO^-$ has two resonating structures
4) The anion is obtained by removal of a proton from the acid molecule

76. In a polar molecule, the ionic charge is 4.8×10^{-10} e.s.u. If the inter ionic distance is 1 Å unit, then the dipole moment is

1) 41.8 debye
2) 4.18 debye
3) 4.8 debye
4) 0.48 debye

77. The electronegativity of A and B are 1.20 and 4.0 respectively. Therefore, ionic character in $A-B$ bond will be

1) 50%
2) 43%
3) 53.3%
4) 72.23%

78. If the dipole moment of toluene and nitro-benzene are 0.43 D and 3.93 D, then what is the expected dipole moment of p-nitro toluene?

1) 3.50 D
2) 2.18 D
3) 4.36 D
4) 5.30 D

79. Which of the following has dipole moment?

1) CO_2
2) p-dichlorobenzene
3) NH_3
4) CH_4

80. The only molecule having dipole moment is

1) 2,2-dimethylpropane
2) *trans*-2-pentene
3) *trans*-3-hexene
4) 2,2,3,3-tetramethylbutane

81. Which one of the following conversions involve change in both hybridisation and shape?

1) $CH_4 \longrightarrow C_2H_6$
2) $NH_3 \longrightarrow NH_4^+$
3) $BF_3 \longrightarrow BF_4^-$
4) $H_2O \longrightarrow H_3O^+$

82. Structure of XeF_5^+ ion is

1) Trigonal bipyramidal
2) Square pyramidal
3) Octahedral
4) Pentagonal

83. The state of hybridisation of S in SF_4 is

1) sp^3 and has a lone pair of electron
2) sp^2 and has tetrahedral structure
3) sp^3d and has a trigonal bipyramidal structure
4) sp^3d^2 and has an octahedral structure

84. Molecular shapes of SF_4, CF_4, XeF_4 are

1) The same with 2, 0 and 1 lone pair of electron respectively
2) The same with 1, 1 and 1 lone pair of electrons respectively
3) Different with 0, 1 and 2 lone pair of electrons respectively
4) Different with 1, 0 and 2 lone pair of electrons respectively
5) Different with 2, 0, 1 lone pair of electron respectively

85. According to VSEPR theory the repulsion between different pair (lone or bond) of electrons obey the order

1) *lp bp lp lp bp bp*
2) *lp bp bp bp lp lp*
3) *lp lp lp bp bp bp*
4) *bp bp lp lp lp bp*

86. Which of the following shows minimum bond angle?
1) H_2O
2) H_2Se
3) H_2S
4) H_2Te

87. Which of the following statements is correct?
1) All carbon to carbon bonds contain a σ - bond and one or more π - bonds
2) All carbon to hydrogen bonds are π - bonds
3) All oxygen to hydrogen bonds are hydrogen bonds
4) All carbon to hydrogen bonds are σ - bonds
5) All carbon to carbon bonds are σ - bonds

88. In BrF_3 molecule, the lone pairs occupy equatorial positions to minimize
1) Lone pair – bond pair repulsion only
2) Bond pair – bond pair repulsion only
3) Lone pair – lone pair repulsion and lone pair – bond pair repulsion
4) Lone pair – lone pair repulsion only

89. Hybridisation of oxygen in diethyl ether is
1) Sp
2) sp^2
3) sp^3
4) sp^3d

90. Number of non-bonding electron pair on Xe in XeF_6, XeF_4 and XeF_2 respectively will be
1) 6, 4, 2
2) 1, 2, 3
3) 3, 2, 1
4) 0, 3, 2

91. Hybridisation of the underline atom changes in
1) $\underline{Al}H_3$ changes to AlH_4^-
2) $H_2\underline{O}$ changes to H_3O^+
3) $\underline{N}H_3$ changes to NH_4^+
4) In all cases

92. The compound 1,2-butadiene has
1) sp, sp^2 and sp^3 hybridised carbon atoms
2) Only sp^2 hybridised carbon atoms
3) Only sp hybridised carbon atoms
4) Only sp and sp^2 hybridised carbon atoms

93. In a regular octahedral molecule, MX_6 the number of $X - M - X$ bonds at 180° is
1) Three
2) Two
3) Six
4) Four

94. Which of the following is correct?
1) The number of electrons present in the valence shell of S in SF_6 is 12.
2) The rates of ionic reactions are very low.
3) According to VSEPR theory, $SnCl_2$ is a linear molecule.
4) The correct order of ability to form ionic compounds among Na^+, Mg^{2+} and Al^{3+} is $Al^{3+} > Mg^{2+} > Na^+$.

95. The percentage of p– character in the orbitals forming P – P bonds in P_4 is
1) 25
2) 33
3) 50
4) 75

Single Correct Answer Type

1   **(4)**

According to Born-Haber cycle the enthalpy of formation (ΔH_f) of an ionic compound may be given as

$$\Delta H_f = S + \frac{1}{2}D + I + E + U$$

Where, I = ionisation energy

S = sublimation energy

E = electron affinity

D = dissociation energy

U = lattice energy of compound

Born-Haber cycle is used to determine the lattice energy of the compound. It also may be used to calculate electron affinity of an element.

2   **(3)**

Potash alum is a double salt.

Potash alum, $K_2SO_4 . Al_x(SO_4)_3 . 24H_2O$ (given)

Ions $AlSO_4$

Valency   +3   -2

Therefore, $Al_3(SO_4)_3$ is compound of Al^{3+} and SO_4^{2-}.

On comparing, x=2

Hence, formula of potash alum is $= K_2SO_4 . Al_2(SO_4)_3 . 24H_2O$

3   **(1)**

Low ionisation potential indicates that element can easily lose electron to form cation.

4   **(4)**

Higher the lattice energy lower the solubility. Out of the four combinations possible, the lattice energy of MgS (bi-bivalent ionic solid) is higher than those of $Na_2S, MgCl_2$ (uni-bivalent or biuni-valent ionic solids) and NaCl (uni-univalent ionic solids) and hence, MgS is the least soluble.

5   **(3)**

Ionic compounds are good conductor of electricity in molten or in solution state. However, they are bad-conductor in solid state.

6   **(2)**

The covalent compounds have low melting point due to weaker forces of attraction among them as compared to strong forces of attraction in ionic compounds.

∵ HCl is covalent compound among CsF, HCl HF and Li

(CsF, HF and LiF are ionic compounds)

∴ HCl has minimum boiling point.

7 **(2)**

$$\frac{1}{2}Cl_2(g) \longrightarrow Cl^-(aq)$$

$$\Delta H = \frac{1}{2}\Delta H_{diss}(Cl_2) + \Delta H_{EA}Cl + \Delta H_{hyd}(Cl^-)$$

$$= \frac{240}{2} - 349 - 381$$

$$= -610 \text{ kJ mol}^{-1}$$

8 **(2)**

Formal charge = Number of electrons in valence shell –

($\frac{1}{2}$ ×numbers of electrons as bond pair+numbers of electrons as lone pair)

$$:\overset{1}{N}=\overset{2}{N}=\overset{3}{N}:$$

For N_1 and N_3

Formal charge = $5 - \left(\frac{4}{2} + 4\right) = 5 - (6) = -1$

For $\quad N_2 = 5 - \frac{1}{2} \times 8 - 0 = 5 - 4 = +1$

9 **(1)**

S has 6 electrons in its the valence shell and it shares 6 electrons with 6 fluorine atoms.

$\therefore$ In SF_6, S has 12 electrons in its valence shell

$$F \times \overset{\overset{\displaystyle F \;\; F}{\times \; \times}}{\underset{\underset{\displaystyle F \;\; F}{\times \; \times}}{\bullet S \bullet}} \times F$$

10 **(3)**

Low ionisation energy indicates that electron can be easily lost and cation formation is easier.

12 **(2)**

(a) **Pauling** gave scale of electronegativity.

(b) **Bronsted** gave concept of acid and base.

(c) **Mullikan** determined charge on electron.

(d) **Lewis** gave electronic theory of bonding.

13 **(5)**

The solubility of a compound mainly depend upon its hydration energy. If the hydration energy of a compound is greater than from its lattice enthalpy, then its is soluble in water. Thus, for solubility

Hydration enthalpy > lattice enthalpy

For compounds P and R hydration enthalpy exceeds the lattice enthalpy, so they are soluble in water.

14   **(2)**

H_2S contain only covalent bonds, as the electronegativity difference between H and S is only $(2.6 - 2.1 = 0.5)$.

15   **(4)**

Metals and non-metals combine to complete their octet. Since, non-metals have lack of electrons, in order to complete their octet, they gain electrons, consequently, the size of non-metal atom will increase.

Metal + Non − metal $\longrightarrow$ Electrovalent bond

$(Na^+)(Cl)$ NaCl

16   **(2)**

A three electrons in its outermost orbit, its valency is 3. B has six electrons in its outermost orbit, its valency is 2

Element

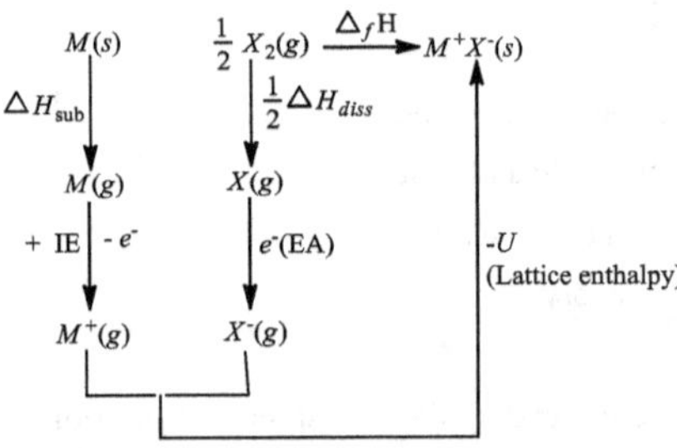

Valency

Formula of the compound $= A_2B_3$

17   **(4)**

During the formation of chemical bond energy decreases

18   **(2)**

The Born-Haber cycle takes place as follows

Hence, Z is M^+X^- (s)

19   **(4)**

Covalent union between two unlike atoms gives rise to the formation of a polar covalent bond in which shared pair of electron shifted towards more electronegative atom. This gives rise to equal but opposite partial charges on two ends. HCl shows polar covalent bond.

20   **(2)**

When there is less difference in electronegativities of two atoms (but electronegativities are not same) and large difference in their size, polar covalent bond forms.

H and Br : Small difference in electronegativities and large difference in size. Hence, form polar covalent bond.

Na and Br : large difference in electronegativities, hence electrovalent bond is formed.

21   **(1)**

Greater the charge, smaller the radius, greater the polarising power and thus greater the covalent nature. This leads to increase in lattice energy.

22   **(1)**

According to Born-lande equation

$$U = \frac{Z^+ Z^- e^2 \mathrm{An}}{r_{\mathrm{node}}}\left(\frac{1}{n} - 1\right)$$

Where , U is lattice energy

r_{node} is interionic distance

$$\because U \propto \frac{1}{\text{interionic disance}}$$

$\therefore$ Ions should be of small size to have high lattice energy.

23   **(1)**

Lewis structure of N_2 molecule is

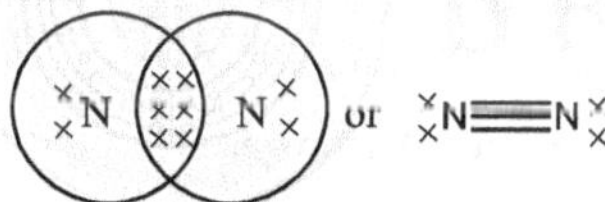

24   **(1)**

The polarising ability is characteristic of cation, smaller the size of cation with large magnitude of positive charge, more will be its polarising ability.

($\because$ It can cause large distortions in anion cloud.)

25   **(3)**

For Be $_n$Al$_2$Si$_6$O$_{18}$

$$2n + 6 + 24 - 36 = 0$$

$n = 3$

26   **(3)**

In all the given compounds, anion is same(Cl^-), hence polarising power is decided by size and charge of cation. Al^{3+} with maximum charge and smallest size has maximum polarising power hence, $AlCl_3$ is maximum covalent.

27   **(3)**

According to Fajan's rule smaller anion is polarised to lesser extent than the larger anion.

∴ compound having smaller anion has more ionic character.

∴ Higher melting

Since, the size of F^- ion is smallest, it is polarised.

∴ AgF will have highest ionic character and hence highest melting point.

(∵ Ionic compounds have greater melting point than covalent compound)

28   **(3)**

According to Fajan's rule, as the size of cation decreases, its polarising power increases. Hence, Cu^{2+} polarise Cl^- ions more than Cu^+. Therefore, $CuCl_2$ has more covalent character and hence, its boiling point is less.

29   **(1)**

Structure of $\overline{N}H_2$ is as follows

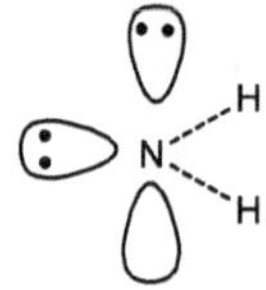

30   **(4)**

The lattice becomes stronger (*i.e.*, the lattice energy U becomes more negative). As r the interionic distance decreases. U is proportional to $\frac{1}{r}$

or
$$U \propto \frac{1}{(r_c + r_a)}$$

31   **(1)**

Total electrons in valence shell of nitrogen and hydrogen.

$$H \overset{\times}{\underset{\bullet}{\cdot}} \overset{\bullet\bullet}{N} \overset{\bullet}{\underset{\overset{\times}{H}}{\cdot}} \times H$$

∴ Total electrons in $NH_3 = 5+1+1+1 = 8$

32   **(4)**

Greater the stability of oxide, greater is the case of its formation. Generally ionic oxides are more stable than covalent oxides and among the given metals only Ca form ionic oxide. Hence, Ca has greater tendency to form oxide.

33   **(2)**

P_4O_6 has following structure.

Thus, every P-atom is linked to 3 oxygen atoms.

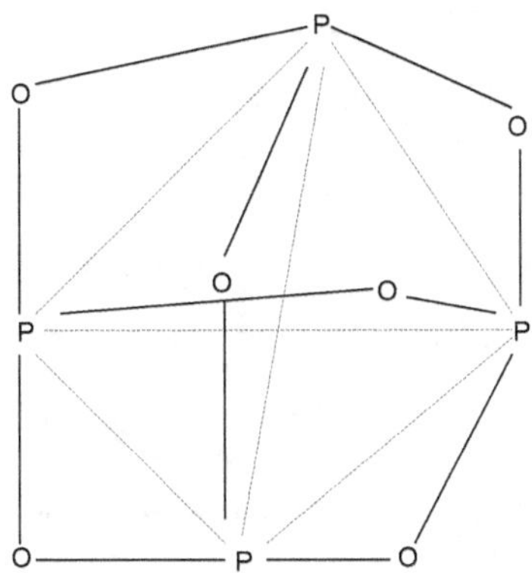

34　　**(2)**

We know that Al^{3+} cation is smaller than Na^+ (because of greater nuclear charge). According to Fajan's rule, small cation polarise anion upto greater extent. Hence, Al^{3+} polarise Cl^- ions upto greater extent, therefore, $AlCl_3$ has covalent bond between Al and Cl atoms.

35　　**(2)**

NH_4Cl contains ionic, covalent and coordinate linkage.

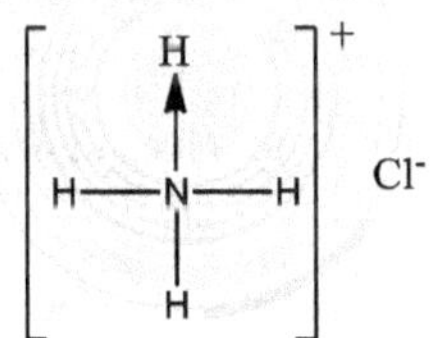

36　　**(1)**

According to Fajan's rule, as the charge on cation increase its size decreases. As a result its tendency to polarise anion increases. This brings more and more covalent character to electrovalent compounds.

∵ Among $AlCl_3$, $LaCl_3$, $MgCl_2$ and $CsCl$ size of Al^{3+} is smallest.

∴ Al^{3+} polarises anion to highest extent.

∴ $AlCl_3$ has maximum covalent character.

37　　**(2)**

The solubility of a compound depends upon its hydration enthalpy. If hydration enthalpy exceeds the lattice enthalpy than it is soluble in water. For Ag_2SO_4, hydration enthalpy is lower than lattice enthalpy, so it is insoluble in water.

38　　**(2)**

For a compound to be soluble, the hydration energy must be greater than the lattice energy.

Since, NaCl is soluble in water but insoluble in benzene.

$$\Delta H_{\text{hydration}} > \Delta H_{\text{lattice energy in water}}$$

and $\Delta H_{\text{hydration}} < \Delta H_{\text{lattice energy in benzene}}$

39 (2)

Coordinate bond is formed.

$(C_2H_5)_2O \longrightarrow BH_3$

$(C_2H_5)_2O$ gives one lone pair of electron to BH_3. So, it is called electron pair donar and BH_3 is called electron pair acceptor.

40 (3)

A coordinate bond is a dative covalent bond in which two atoms form bond and one of them provides both electrons.

$$X:+Y \longrightarrow X:Y \ or \ X \longrightarrow Y$$

41 (4)

Chile salt petre ($NaNO_3$), potash alum

($K_2SO_4. Al_2(SO_4)_3. 24H_2O$) and green vitriol ($FeSO_4. 7H_2O$)are ionic compounds. They produce ions in their aqueous solutions, so they are conducting in nature. Ethyl alcohol, C_2H_5OH being covalent in nature, does not produce any ion in aqueous solution. Hence, it is non-conducting in nature.

42 (1)

Ionic compounds break into their constituent ions when dissolved in water.

Carnallite is double salt having composition,

$KCl. MgCl_2. 6H_2O$. It gives K^+, Cl^- and Mg^{2+}ions when dissolved in water.

43 (4)

$H_2C = C = CH_2$ or
Allene (C_3H_4)

$$\begin{matrix} & & H & H & \\ & & | & | & \\ H - C & = & C & = & C - H \end{matrix}$$

It has 2 double and 4 single bonds

44 (3)

In NaOH, Na^+ and OH^- ions are bonded together by ionic bond while in OH^- ion oxygen and hydrogen atoms are bonded together by covalent bond $Na^+[O - H]^-$.

45 (1)

Valencies of X, Y and Z is +2, +2 and -2 respectively so, they will form a compound having of formula XYZ_2.

46 (1)

Proton number does not change in ion formation, though number of electrons and size change during this.

47   **(2)**

Diamond has a three-dimensional structure in which a large number of carbon atoms are arranged tetrahedrally by covalent bonds. It is an allotropic form of carbon.

48   **(2)**

Metals are more electropositive and lose electrons, while non – metals have tendency to gain electron.

49   **(3)**

Higher the charge/size ratio, more is the polarising power.

$$K^+ < Ca^{2+} < Mg^{2+} < Be^{2+}$$

50   **(1)**

The melting point of naphthalene is minimum because it is non – polar covalent compound and has less melting point.

51   **(1)**

C – Cl bond is more ionic than C – I bond because of the greater difference in electronegativities of C and Cl as compared to that of carbon and iodine. Therefore, C – Cl bond is stronger than C – I bond.

52   **(4)**

Given,

observed dipole moment $= 1.03$ D

Bond length of HCl molecule, $d = 1.275$ Å

$$= 1.275 \times 10^{-8}\,\text{cm}$$

Charge of electron, $e^- = 4.8 \times 10^{-10}\,\text{esu}$

Percentage ionic character $= ?$

Theoretical value of dipole moment $= e \times d$

$$= 4.8 \times 10^{-10} \times 1.275 \times 10^{-8}\,\text{esu.cm}$$

$$= 6.12 \times 10^{-18}\,\text{esu.cm}$$

$$= 6.12\ \text{D}$$

Percentage ionic character

$$= \frac{\text{observed dipole moment}}{\text{theoretical value of dipole moment}} \times 100$$

$$= \frac{1.03}{6.12} \times 100 = 16.83\%$$

53   **(1)**

CCl_4 and ![Cl—(benzene ring)—Cl] compounds has zero dipole moment due to their symmetrical structure.

54   **(3)**

Per cent ionic character is given by % of ionic character.

$$= 16(X_A - X_B) + 3.5(X_A - X_B)^2$$

From the above relation, it is clear that as soon as $(X_A - X_B)$ increases, % ionic character will also increase.

Therefore, curve C shows a correct path.

55   **(3)**

The molecules having distorted geometry have dipole moment and those having regular geometry have zero dipole moment.

$\because$ NH_3, CH_3Cl and ClO_2 have distorted geometry.

$\therefore$ They have dipole moment.

$\because$ BF_3 has regular triangular planar geometry.

The dipole moment of BF_3 is zero.

56   **(2)**

Calculated dipole moment,

$$\mu_{cal} = 2.0 \times 10^{-10} \text{ m} \times 1.6 \times 10^{-19} \text{ C}$$

$$= 3.2 \times 10^{-29} \text{ C} - \text{m.}$$

Percentage of ionic character $= \dfrac{\mu_{exp}}{\mu_{cal}} \times 100$

$$= \frac{5.12 \times 10^{-29}}{3.2 \times 10^{-29}} \times 100 = 16\%$$

57   **(4)**

Molecules in *trans*-1, 2-dichloroethene are symmetrical hence, no dipole moment.

58   **(4)**

CCl_4 does not exhibit dipole moment due to its symmetrical structure.

$$\begin{array}{c} Cl \\ | \\ Cl - C - Cl \\ | \\ Cl \end{array}$$

59   **(2)**

Charge of $e^- = 1.6 \times 10^{-19}$

Dipole moment of HBr $= 1.6 \times 10^{-30}$

Inter-atomic spacing $= 1$ Å

$$= 1 \times 10^{-10} \text{m}$$

Percentage of ionic character in HBr

$$= \frac{\text{Dipole moment of HBr} \times 100}{\text{inter spacing distance} \times q}$$

$$= \frac{1.6 \times 10^{-30}}{1.6 \times 10^{-19} \times 10^{-10}} \times 100$$

$$= 10^{-30} \times 10^{29} \times 100$$

$$= 10^{-1} \times 100$$

$$= 0.1 \times 100$$

$$= 10\%$$

60   **(2)**

A symmetrical molecule have zero dipole moment. The dipole moment of BF_3 molecule is zero due to its symmetrical (triangular planar) structure.

The three fluoride atoms lie at the corners of an equilateral triangle with boron at the centre. Thus, the vectorial addition of the dipole moments of the three bonds gives a net sum of zero.

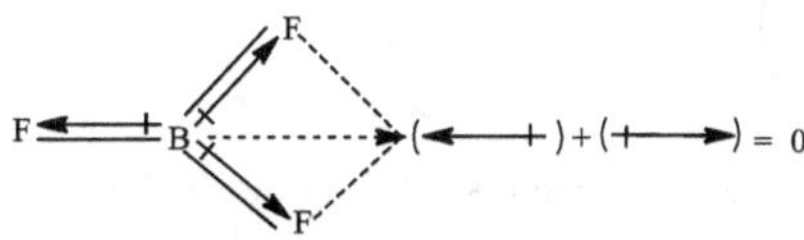

61   **(3)**

NO_2 and O_3 both are having irregular geometry.

62   **(4)**

$$\text{Covalent character} \propto \frac{1}{\text{size of cation}}$$

$$\propto \text{size of anion}$$

(according to Fajan's rule)

Lower the covalent character, higher will be ionic character.

Cl_2O, contains O^{2-}, NCl_3 contains N^{3-}

, $PbCl_2$ contains Pb^{2+} and $BaCl_2$ contains Ba^{2+}.

Hence, the order of covalent character is

$$NCl_3 > Cl_2O > PbCl_2 > BaCl_2$$

$\therefore BaCl_2$ has the greatest ionic character.

63   **(3)**

μ experimental = Dipole moment $\times 10^{-18}$

μ theoretical = Bond length $\times 4.8 \times 10^{-10}$ esu $\times$ cm

$$\text{Percentage ionic character} = \frac{\mu_{\text{experimental}}}{\mu_{\text{theoretical}}} \times 100$$

$$= \frac{1.0 \times 10^{-18} \times 100}{1.25 \times 4.8 \times 10^{-10} \times 10^{-8}}$$

$$= 16.66\%$$

64   **(4)**

Usually symmetrical molecules have less dipole moment in comparison to unsymmetrical molecules.

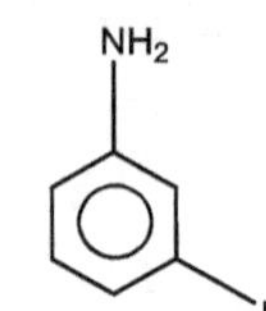

Hence,  NO_2 (*m*-nitroaniline) has the highest dipole moment among the given.

65   **(3)**

Number of bonds between two atoms is called bond order.

Resonating structures of benzene are

∴ In benzene, the carbon – carbon bond is between the double and single bond due to the resonance, so its bond order is 1.5.

66   **(3)**

$CHCl_3$ molecule has largest dipole moment among the given species.

67   **(2)**

I has maximum covalent bond and negative charge on electronegative nitrogen, most stable. III has more covalent bond than both II and IV, III is second most stable. Between II and IV, II is more stable since it has negative charge on nitrogen while IV has negative charge carbon.

68   **(1)**

Percentage ionic character

$$= \frac{\text{experimental value of DM}}{\text{theoretical value of DM}} \times 100$$

$$= \frac{1.03}{6.12} \times 100 = 17\%$$

69   **(2)**

The zero dipole moment of BF_3 molecule is due to its symmetrical (triangular planar) structure.

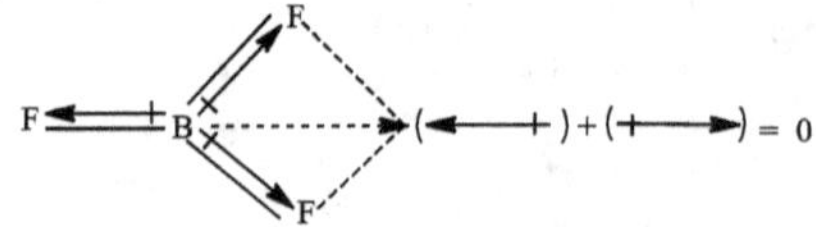

70 **(2)**

The molecule of N_2O is linear as would be expected for a triatomic molecule with 16 outer shell electrons. Its resonance structure is

71 **(1)**

The dipole moment of a polar molecule depends upon its geometry. A symmetrical molecule is non-polar even though it contain polar bonds. Methane molecule (CH_4) has zero moment value of dipole moment due to its symmetrical structure.

In $CHCl_3$, the resultant of C – H and C – Cl dipole oppose the resultant of two C – Cl dipoles while in CH_2Cl_2, the resultant of C – H dipoles adds to resultant of two C – Cl. In case CH_3Cl, the resultant of two C – H dipole adds to the resultant of two C – Cl. In case CH_3Cl the resultant of two C – H dipoles add to the resultant of C – H and C – Cl dipoles.

Thus dipole moment of CH_3Cl is highest among the given compounds. The molecule (CCl_4) again becomes symmetrical and dipole moment reduces to zero.

72 **(1)**

The molecule in which the bond dipoles of all the bonds are cancel out by each other, is called non – polar *e.g.*, CCl_4.

InCCl_4, there is a large difference between the electronegativities of C and Cl but all the four C – Cl bond dipoles cancel each other , hence it is a non polar molecule.

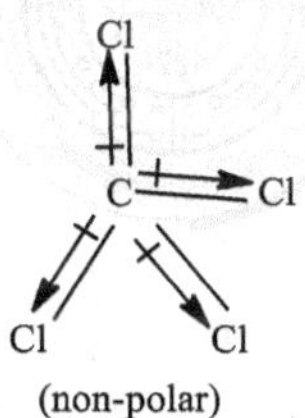

(non-polar)

73 **(1)**

The molecules having no difference in electronegativity of bonded atoms are non-polar in nature. They are molecules having same atoms.

∴ Among HCl, HF, HBr and H_2. H_2 is non-polar molecule.

74 **(3)**

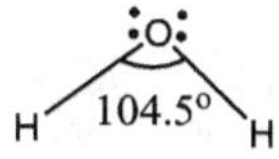

In water molecule the H – O – H bond angle is 104.5° and dipole moment is 1.84 D.

The bond angle of H_2O is lower than 109.28″ due to the presence of two lone pair of electrons on the oxygen atom.

76   **(3)**

Given ionic charge $= 4.8 \times 10^{-10}$ e.s.u. and ionic distance $= 1\text{Å} = 10^{-8}$ cm. We know that dipole moment = Ionic charge × ionic distance

$$= (4.8 \times 10^{-10}) \times 10^{-8}$$

$= 4.8 \times 10^{-18}$ e. s. u. per cm

$= 4.8$ debye.

77   **(4)**

Ionic character$= 16(E_A - E_B) + 3.5(E_A - E_B)^2$

$$= 16(4 - 1.2) + 3.5(4 - 1.2)^2$$

$$= 72.24\%$$

78   **(3)**

Methyl group has $+I$ effect and $-NO_2$ group has $-I$ effect. Therefore, in *p*-nitro toluene the dipole moments of $-CH_3$ and $-NO_2$ groups act in the same direction. So, the resultant dipole moment is additive.

i.e., 3.93+0.43=4.36 debye

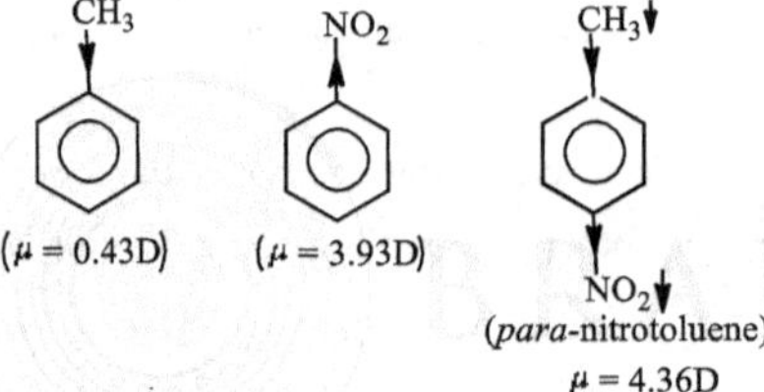

79   **(3)**

Dipole moment is a vector quantity. The dipole moment of symmetrical molecule is zero. Only the molecule which has distorted shape has dipole moment.

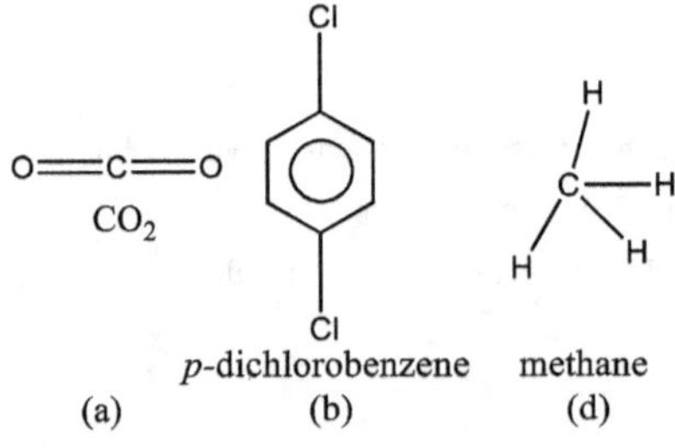

$\because$ CO$_2$, *p*-dichlorobenzene and CH$_4$ have regular symmetrical shape.

$\therefore$ They don't have dipole moment.

$$H-\underset{\underset{\displaystyle H}{|}}{\overset{\displaystyle \cdot\cdot}{N}}-H$$

(NH$_3$)

(c)

NH$_3$ has distorted structure due to presence of lone pair of electron.

∴ It has dipole moment.

80   **(2)**

Trans 2-pentene has dipole moment.

$$\underset{H}{\overset{H_3C}{>}}C=C\underset{CH_2CH_3}{\overset{H}{<}}$$

Because $+I$ effect of ethyl group is more than that of CH$_3$ group, hence the two dipoles do not cancel each other.

81   **(3)**

(a) CH$_4$ $\longrightarrow$ CH$_3$ $-$ CH$_3$

    $4bp+0lp$ $4bp4bp$

Hybridisation $sp^3 sp^3 sp^3$

Structure tetrahedral tetrahedral

(b) NH$_3$ $\longrightarrow$ NH$_4^+$

$3bp+1lp$ $4bp$

Hybridisation $sp^3 sp^3$

Structure pyramidal tetrahedral

(c) BF$_3$ $\longrightarrow$ BF$_4^-$

$3bp$ $4bp$

Hybridisation $sp^2 sp^3$

Structure trigonal   tetrahedral

 planar

(d) H$_2$O $\longrightarrow$ H$_3$O$^+$

$2bp+2lp$ $3bp+1lp$

Hybridisation $sp^3 sp^3$

Structure angular pyramidal

Thus conversion of BF$_3$ into BF$_4^-$ involves change in both hybridisation and shape.

82   **(2)**

In XeF$_5^+$, Xe atom has only seven electrons , *i.e.*, $5s^2\,5p^5$. Here two $5p$ electrons are promoted to $5d$-sublevel. Then $5s$, three $5p$ and two $5d$ orbitals hybridize to give six sp^3d^2 hybrid orbitals in an octahedral geometry. Out of these five orbitals are singly occupied which form sigma bonds with five F atoms. The sixth hybrid orbital is occupied by a lone pair in *trans* position giving a square pyramid structure.

83　(3)

S in SF_4 possesses trigonal bipyramidal structure with sp^3d hybridisation.

S in ground state

S in ground state

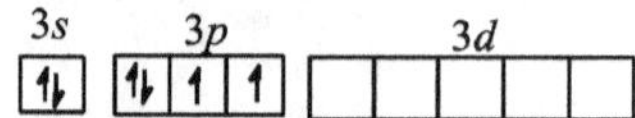

S in excited state

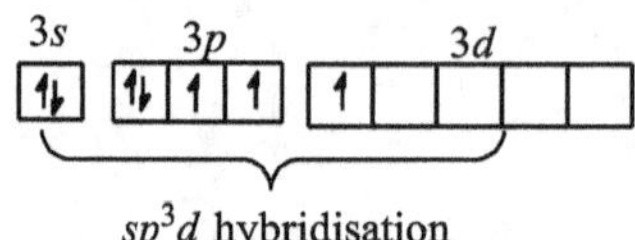

sp^3d hybridisation

S in excited state

84　(4)

Molecular shapes of SF_4, CF_4, XeF_4 are different with 1, 0 and 2 lone pair or electrons respectively.

85　(3)

According to valence shell electron pair repulsion (VSEPR) theory, the order of repulsive interactions between various electron is

$$lp - lp > lp - bp > bp - bp$$

86　(4)

Hybride :　　H_2O　H_2S　H_2Se　　H_2Te

Bond angle : 104°　92°　91°　　90°

In all of the given species central atom is sp^3 hybridised. They have angular shape due to the presence of two lone pair of electron. The bond angle decreases with decrease in electronegativity therefore H_2Te shows minimum bond angle.

87　(4)

All carbon to hydrogen bonds are σ-bonds

88　(4)

In BrF_3 molecule, Br is sp^3d hybrid, but geometry is T-shaped due to distortion of geometry from trigonal-bipyramidal to T-shaped by the involvement of lone pair-lone pair repulsion.
Here
$lp - lp$ repulsion $= 0$
$lp - bp$ repulsion $= 4$
$bp - bp$ repulsion $= 2$

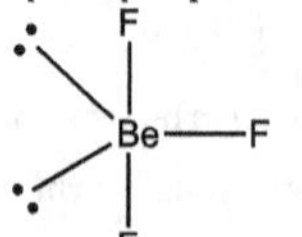

89 **(3)**

In diethyl ether oxygen undergoes sp^3 hybridisation forming four sp^3 hybrid orbitals.

91 **(1)**

In AlH_3, Al is sp^2 hybridised while in AlH_4^-, Al is sp^3 hybridised.

92 **(1)**

1, 2-butandiene has the structure.

$$H - C - C = C = C - H$$

with H H H bonds and $sp^3\,sp^2\,sp\,sp^2$

93 **(1)**

In octahedral structure MX_6, the six hybrid orbitals (sp^3d^2) are directed towards the corners of a regular octahedral with an angle of 90°. According to following structure of MX_6 the number of $X - M - X$ bonds at 180° must be three.

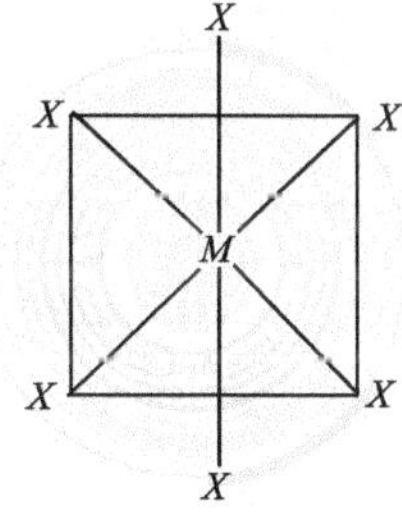

94 **(1)**

SF_6 does not obey octet rule as in it S-atom has 12 electrons in its valence shell.

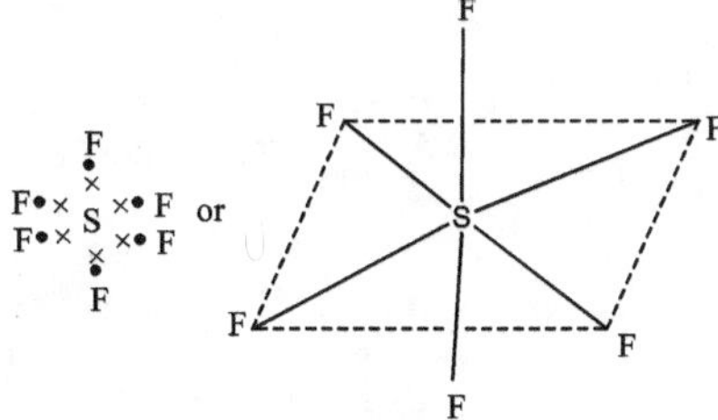

95 **(4)**

Phosphorus atom is sp^3 hybridised in P_4 usually. Therefore, p-character 75%